Learning Spring Boot

Learn how to use Spring Boot to build apps
faster than ever before

Greg L. Turnquist

D1520441

BIRMINGHAM - MUMBAI

Learning Spring Boot

First published: November 2014

Production reference: 1211114

Published by Packt Publishing Ltd.
Livery Place
35 Livery Street
Birmingham B3 2PB, UK.

ISBN 978-1-78439-302-1

www.packtpub.com

Credits

Author
Greg L. Turnquist

Reviewers
Zoltan Altfatter
Roy Clarkson
Theo Pack
Marco Vermeulen
Geoffroy Warin
Ricky Yim

Commissioning Editor
Dipika Gaonkar

Acquisition Editor
Owen Roberts

Content Development Editor
Anila Vincent

Technical Editors
Vivek Arora
Siddhi Rane
Shruti Rawool

Copy Editors
Relin Hedly
Stuti Srivastava

Project Coordinator
Neha Bhatnagar

Proofreaders
Simran Bhogal
Lawrence A. Herman

Indexer
Hemangini Bari

Production Coordinator
Nitesh Thakur

Cover Work
Nitesh Thakur

Foreword

People often ask about the origins of the Spring Boot project. The truth is that there are many origins, but there was a need for something to be done in this space, and at the time we started work on it in late 2012 or early 2013, the world was ready for it. There is one feature request (`https://jira.spring.io/browse/SPR-9888`) of the Spring Framework that is often quoted as a kick-starter and was indeed significant in gathering the impetus required to start work on Boot. However, the story goes further back and has quite a few strands that need to be woven together before you can see the whole picture.

When we were first getting Spring Batch ready for a release in early 2007, we added a class with a `main()` method (`CommandLineJobRunner`) because there was, and still is, a lot of demand to run batch jobs in their own processes. When I was working a lot with the banks and financial institutions in London in the late noughties, the same requirement to run Spring as an application from the command line came up over and over. The Spring Batch use case was always there, but more often, this was in the context of standalone message listeners. Of course, everyone ended up writing their own mini platform in order to launch Spring from the command line. Another Spring Framework feature request that refers to this problem can be found at `https://jira.spring.io/browse/SPR-8077`. Going back to demos I created with Mark Fisher at SpringOne in 2009, I had some utilities that could embed Tomcat as a server in a Spring application, which is somewhat connected to this work.

So, getting a Spring application off the ground in its own process was one driver for Spring Boot, and coupled with the ability to optionally embed a servlet container, it became quite a powerful combination on its own. Another factor, though—and somewhat independent—is the set of features that were unlocked by Phil Webb's contribution of the `@Conditional` annotation to the Spring Framework in 4.0. The `@Conditional` annotation is a fairly simple idea, and it is an obvious generalization of a feature (`@Profile`) that had been in Spring since Version 3.1; however, the power that it unlocks is amazing and is truly instrumental in the success of Spring Boot as it stands today.

The basic `@Conditional` machinery is in the Spring Framework (and might well be enhanced in Version 4.2), but the most avid consumer of it and what unleashed all this power is the Spring Boot auto-configuration module and its `@EnableAutoConfiguration` annotation. Without this and its emphasis on being opinionated, on convention over configuration, and more importantly, on getting out of the way if the user wants to have their own opinion, Spring Boot would not be what it is today.

A third major input of the Spring Boot project in its early phases was what we might now (and in the early phases) call the DevOps movement; this reflects the many requirements of real people running real applications in production going back further than Spring Boot and even Spring itself. There are many good reasons why sharing responsibilities between developers and operators makes sense, and we can't cover them here, but the important thing is that many (probably all) of the Spring Engineering team members have real-life experience running Spring applications in production at various places and various stages in their careers. At the time we started work on Spring Boot, this was particularly useful for me as I had just come out of the Cloud Foundry team where I was part of a group that built and ran the identity management part of the platform known as the UAA server (`https://github.com/cloudfoundry/uaa`), which was all written using Spring. This wasn't my only experience running Spring applications, but it was the immediate one, and we used metrics and management endpoints to get visibility in the running process. This is vital for operators, whether or not they are developers, and furthermore, many of the requirements are ubiquitous and can be provided once rather than having to be reinvented everywhere; these are the features that made up Spring Boot Actuator.

There is more to Spring Boot than just main methods, embedded containers, auto-configuration, and management endpoints. (The pure joy of getting started with a fully featured Spring application in a few lines of code cannot be understated, for instance.) Instead of trying to list them all here, I invite you to take a dip into this book, break out an editor or an IDE, and crank up some applications for yourself. Greg Turnquist has done a fantastic job of introducing the basic tenets of Spring Boot with loads of code to look at and copy from. One of the most refreshing and exciting aspects of working with Spring Boot has been the enthusiasm with which it has been received and embraced by the Spring Engineering team, by the wider community, and the number of people who have found the time to contribute to the project (we had around 90 committers as of the 1.1.6 release in late summer 2014). Greg has been an important member of the Spring Boot team despite having a day job doing other things in Spring Engineering, and we are grateful for that as well as the effort he has obviously lavished on this excellent book. Reading and enjoying coding with Spring has never been so much fun!

Dave Syer
Senior Engineering Consultant and Co-lead for Spring Boot

About the Author

Greg L. Turnquist has developed software professionally since 1997. From 2002 to 2010, he was part of the senior software team that worked on Harris' $3.5 billion FAA telco program, architecting mission-critical enterprise apps while managing a software team. He provided after-hours support to a nation-wide telco system and is no stranger to midnight failures and software triages. In 2010, he joined the SpringSource division of VMware, which was spun off into Pivotal in 2013.

As a test-bitten script junky, Java geek, and JavaScript Padawan, he is a member of the Spring Data team as well as the mobile-oriented Allspark team. He has made key contributions to Spring Boot and Spring Data REST while also serving as Getting Started Guides, editor-at-large for `http://spring.io/`. He has migrated Spring Data release train's entire reference docs to Asciidoctor in a week. He has also contributed to multiple Spring portfolio projects.

He has worked with Java, Spring, Spring Security, AspectJ, and Jython technologies and has also developed sophisticated scripts for *nix and Windows platforms. As a wiki evangelist, he has also deployed a LAMP-based wiki website that provides fingertip knowledge to users.

In 2006, Greg created the Spring Python project. The Spring Framework provided many useful features, and he wanted these features to be available when he was working with Python. He has written *Python Testing Cookbook* and *Spring Python 1.1* for Packt Publishing.

He has completed a Master's degree in Computer Engineering at Auburn University and lives in the United States with his family.

About the Reviewers

Zoltan Altfatter (@altfatterz) is a true craftsman who specializes in custom development using Java and related open source frameworks. He is a certified Spring Professional who loves and knows how to build scalable software products. He values simplicity; however, he is not afraid to debug complex problems. He learns fast and enjoys sharing his knowledge at tech meetups or through his blogs (http://altfatterz.blogspot.nl). He has experience in several sectors, including finance and telecom, and has worked at big consultancy firms, middle-size companies, and small startups. He is passionate about JVM, REST, reactive systems, and PaaS solutions.

Roy Clarkson is a Java geek, Spring expert, project lead for Spring for Android and Spring Mobile. He graduated from Georgia Tech. He joined VMware in 2010, and then was spun off into Pivotal's startup in 2013. He loves to run and to drink coffee. He lives in the United States with his family.

Theo Pack is a software engineer who has several years of experience in developing frontend and backend applications. He has completed his MSc and has been working at Cologne Intelligence GmbH, which is a consulting company in Germany, since 2009.

He is passionate about technology and likes to master new programming languages. You can visit his blog at http://furikuri.github.io or follow him on Twitter at @furikuri.

Marco Vermeulen is a South African software developer who lives and works in London. He is passionate about writing well-crafted code that is driven and guided by tests.

As a proponent of BDD, he has successfully applied this technique in enterprise as well as on open source projects. In his spare time, he contributes to OSS. He is the creator of the GVM (Groovy enVironment Manager).

He also regularly speaks at conferences, and has spoken at Spring One 2GX, Gr8Conf EU, Gr8Conf US, Grails eXchange, and Greach in past years.

Geoffroy Warin has been programming since he was 10. He is a firm believer in the software craftsmanship movement and open source initiatives. He is a developer by choice and conviction, and has been working on the conception of enterprise-level web applications in Java and JavaScript throughout his career.

He teaches courses on Java web stacks and is a Groovy and Spring enthusiast.

You can find more about him on his blog at `http://geowarin.github.io` and on Twitter at `https://twitter.com/geowarin`.

Ricky Yim is a passionate software engineer who has over 15 years of industry experience. He is a firm believer in using test-driven and behavior-driven development and agile practices to solve problems. He takes a flexible approach to software delivery and applies innovative solutions. He is currently a Principal Consultant and also the Delivery Manager for DiUS Computing, Sydney, Australia.

You can find out more about him here at `http://codingricky.com` and on Twitter at `https://twitter.com/codingricky`.

www.PacktPub.com

Support files, eBooks, discount offers, and more

For support files and downloads related to your book, please visit www.PacktPub.com.

Did you know that Packt offers eBook versions of every book published, with PDF and ePub files available? You can upgrade to the eBook version at www.PacktPub.com and as a print book customer, you are entitled to a discount on the eBook copy. Get in touch with us at service@packtpub.com for more details.

At www.PacktPub.com, you can also read a collection of free technical articles, sign up for a range of free newsletters and receive exclusive discounts and offers on Packt books and eBooks.

https://www2.packtpub.com/books/subscription/packtlib

Do you need instant solutions to your IT questions? PacktLib is Packt's online digital book library. Here, you can search, access, and read Packt's entire library of books.

Why subscribe?

- Fully searchable across every book published by Packt
- Copy and paste, print, and bookmark content
- On demand and accessible via a web browser

Free access for Packt account holders

If you have an account with Packt at www.PacktPub.com, you can use this to access PacktLib today and view 9 entirely free books. Simply use your login credentials for immediate access.

Table of Contents

Preface

Back in 2012, a couple of Spring developers stepped back from the current state of Java development and asked some questions, "Developers with Spring MVC on the classpath probably want to use it. How can we make this easier?" "How can we make Spring more accessible to new developers?" "Why does a computer student have to learn about build systems, web.xml files, and all the other steps to simply display "Hello, World" on a web page?"

By approaching the topic of simplifying development without sacrificing the power of Spring, they coded several powerful features. At the SpringOne conference in 2013, they unveiled Spring Boot with its ability to auto-configure Spring Beans, configure things with simple property management, and run apps inside an embedded Tomcat container bundled inside a runnable JAR file. They also showed Spring Boot's opinionated approach to pick which Spring beans were configured based on classpath settings among other factors.

The response was incredible. The session by Phil Webb and Dave Syer witnessed record attendance along with lots of follow-up questions. (I know because I was there.) People were discussing it in the hallways between talks. The ensuing stream of blog articles after the conference from the Spring community was relentless. Proof of its success and staying power was further evidenced at the 2014 SpringOne conference a year later. Spring Boot had woven itself into almost every Java-based demo as a new lingua franca among Spring developers.

The keynote presented by Andy Glover, a NetFlix engineer who had once developed Java but left to write Ruby on Rails, explained the reasons why he returned to Java. Spring Boot made Java fun again! Furthermore, when a contingent of over 20 Spring developers from the conference visited the Java Metroplex Users Group in Dallas the same week, there was a lot of excitement. Lots of questions were fired off to the Spring team with many about Spring Boot, including "When will there be a book about Spring Boot?"

I hope you enjoy this experience.

What this book covers

Chapter 1, Quick Start with Groovy, explains how to rapidly craft a Spring MVC app that runs inside an embedded Tomcat container using just a few lines of Groovy and no build file. You will also learn how to plug in jQuery, web templates, and production-grade metrics and health checks.

Chapter 2, Quick Start with Java, explains how to rapidly create a Spring MVC app with Java that connects to GitHub and scans for open issues using Spring Social GitHub. Then create a mobile frontend and deploy it to the cloud.

Chapter 3, Debugging and Managing Your App, explains how to create a JMS-based publisher/subscriber app with embedded ActiveMQ that simulates ops center monitoring. You will learn how Spring Boot auto-configures things as well as how to override its opinion with your own. Also, you can add customized health checks and custom metrics, and reconfigure Spring Boot's default management settings.

Chapter 4, Data Access with Spring Boot, explains how to spin up a sports team app backed by a relational database using Spring Data JPA. You will see how to use Spring Boot's support of Spring profiles to have an in-memory database for development while switching to a persistent one for production. You will also discover how Spring Boot auto-configures database support. You will learn how to export the database layer with Spring Data REST as a hypermedia-based RESTful interface based on several REST standards. Finally, you will get a taste of switching to Spring Data MongoDB.

Chapter 5, Securing Your App with Spring Boot, explains how to create a fully functional sports-team roster app with Spring MVC and then secure it with Spring Security. You will also learn how to control security through both URL and method-level rules. Next, you will discover how to configure Spring Boot's embedded Tomcat servlet container to also serve things via SSL. This chapter also explains how to fine-tune your security policies to force traffic over encrypted channels to protect user data by default.

What you need for this book

Spring Boot supports Java 6 and higher, but all code examples in this book are based on Java 8.

Spring Boot doesn't require a build system, but this book uses Gradle. Gradle comes with a wrapper (`http://www.gradle.org/docs/current/userguide/gradle_wrapper.html`), meaning you don't need a particular version. It is recommended that you install the latest version of Gradle available to configure wrappers. More details on using the wrapper are offered later in this book.

Some parts of this book use Bower to install JavaScript modules. To use it, please visit `http://bower.io`.

Parts of this book use ActiveMQ (`http://activemq.apache.org`), MySQL (`http://www.mysql.com`), and MongoDB (`http://www.mongodb.org`).

Spring Boot has Groovy support (refer to *Chapter 1, Quick Start with Groovy*), but comes with an embedded Groovy compiler, so you don't have to install Groovy on your system.

If you use Mac, you might want to investigate Homebrew (`http://brew.sh`) as an alternative package manager for certain utilities used in this book.

Who this book is for

This book is aimed to help developers who are new to Spring Boot get up and running quickly in the arena of Spring app development. It is also for experienced Spring developers, as it shows how to remove low-level boilerplate and instead focus on building functional apps while learning how to override Boot's opinion.

Conventions

In this book, you will find a number of styles of text that distinguish between different kinds of information. Here are some examples of these styles, and an explanation of their meaning.

Code words in text, database table names, folder names, filenames, file extensions, pathnames, dummy URLs, user input, and Twitter handles are shown as follows: "A Spring MVC app is marked by the `@Controller` annotation."

A block of code is set as follows:

```
@RestController
class App {
    @RequestMapping("/")
    def home() {
        "Hello, world!"
    }
}
```

When we wish to draw your attention to a particular part of a code block, the relevant lines or items are set in bold:

```
@RestController
class App {
    @RequestMapping("/")
    def home() {
        "Hello, world!"
    }
}
```

Any command-line input or output is written as follows:

```
$ spring run app.groovy
```

New terms and **important words** are shown in bold. Words that you see on the screen, in menus or dialog boxes, for example, appear in the text like this: "Click on **Generate new token.**"

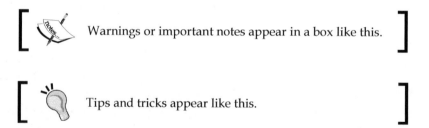

Warnings or important notes appear in a box like this.

Tips and tricks appear like this.

Reader feedback

Feedback from our readers is always welcome. Let us know what you think about this book—what you liked or may have disliked. Reader feedback is important for us to develop titles that you really get the most out of. To send us general feedback, simply send an e-mail to feedback@packtpub.com, and mention the book title via the subject of your message.

If there is a topic that you have expertise in and you are interested in either writing or contributing to a book, see our author guide on http://www.packtpub.com/authors.

Customer support

Now that you are the proud owner of a Packt book, we have a number of things to help you to get the most from your purchase.

Downloading the example code

You can download the example code files for all Packt books you have purchased from your account at http://www.packtpub.com. If you purchased this book elsewhere, you can visit http://www.packtpub.com/support and register to have the files e-mailed directly to you.

You can also download the example code files for this book from GitHub at https://github.com/gregturn/learning-spring-boot-code.

Errata

Although we have taken every care to ensure the accuracy of our content, mistakes do happen. If you find a mistake in one of our books—maybe a mistake in the text or the code—we would be grateful if you would report this to us. By doing so, you can save other readers from frustration and help us improve subsequent versions of this book. If you find any errata, please report them by visiting http://www.packtpub.com/submit-errata, selecting your book, clicking on the **Errata Submission Form** link, and entering the details of your errata. Once your errata are verified, your submission will be accepted and the errata will be uploaded on our website, or added to any list of existing errata, under the Errata section of that title.

To view the previously submitted errata, go to https://www.packtpub.com/books/content/support and enter the name of the book in the search field. The required information will appear under the Errata section.

Piracy

Piracy of copyright material on the Internet is an ongoing problem across all media. At Packt, we take the protection of our copyright and licenses very seriously. If you come across any illegal copies of our works, in any form, on the Internet, please provide us with the location address or website name immediately so that we can pursue a remedy.

Please contact us at `copyright@packtpub.com` with a link to the suspected pirated material.

We appreciate your help in protecting our authors, and our ability to bring you valuable content.

Questions

You can contact us at `questions@packtpub.com` if you are having a problem with any aspect of the book, and we will do our best to address it.

1
Quick Start with Groovy

"Working with Spring Boot is like pair-programming with the Spring developers."

— Josh Long `@starbuxman`

This chapter introduces Spring Boot using the deft programming language of Groovy. If you're not interested in Groovy, you can enjoy a similar high-speed experience with pure Java in the next chapter.

In this chapter, we will cover the following topics:

- Creating a full-blown Spring MVC web app with just a few lines of code
- Seeing how to install Spring Boot's simple CLI
- Learning how to write automated tests with both JUnit and Spock
- Bundling up the application as a runnable JAR file
- Ramping up our app to use templates and jQuery
- Adding production-ready support such as metrics, health, environment, and other things with a single line of code

Getting started

Spring Boot lets us rapidly create rock solid applications. As an example, look at the following source code written in Groovy in `app.groovy`:

```groovy
@RestController
class App {
    @RequestMapping("/")
    def home() {
        "Hello, world!"
    }
}
```

Believe it or not, this small chunk of code is a complete, runnable web application with the details shown as follows:

- The `@RestController` annotation asks Spring MVC to look for web routes. This annotation also indicates that every HTTP endpoint in this class will write its results directly into the HTTP response instead of using a view.

- The `@RequestMapping` annotation maps the `home()` method to the / route. (By the way, it doesn't really matter what the method is named.)

- In Groovy, the final statement is the return value, so, there's no need to type `return`.

- Also, we don't have to tag either the class or the method as `public`, and we can drop the semicolons, which really trims away the cruft.

Let's launch this app using Spring Boot's `spring` tool, aka the **Command Line Interface** (CLI) tool as shown here, and see what it produces. (I promise we'll see how to install it later in this chapter.)

```
$ spring run app.groovy
```

The output for the preceding command will be as follows:

```
  .   ____          _            __ _ _
 /\\ / ___'_ __ _ _(_)_ __  __ _ \ \ \ \
( ( )\___ | '_ | '_| | '_ \/ _` | \ \ \ \
 \\/  ___)| |_)| | | | | || (_| |  ) ) ) )
  '  |____| .__|_| |_|_| |_\__, | / / / /
 =========|_|==============|___/=/_/_/_/
 :: Spring Boot ::        (v1.1.6.RELEASE)


2014-06-11 22:50:24.435 ... : Starting application on retina with PID
55927 (/...
2014-06-11 22:50:24.610 ... : Refreshing org.springframework.boot.
context.embe...
2014-06-11 22:50:25.194 ... : Overriding bean definition for bean
'beanNameVie...
2014-06-11 22:50:26.027 ... : Server initialized with port: 8080
2014-06-11 22:50:26.249 ... : Starting service Tomcat
```

```
2014-06-11 22:50:26.249 ... : Starting Servlet Engine: Apache
Tomcat/7.0.54

2014-06-11 22:50:26.343 ... : Unknown loader org.springframework.boot.
cli.comp...

2014-06-11 22:50:26.349 ... : Initializing Spring embedded
WebApplicationContext

2014-06-11 22:50:26.349 ... : Root WebApplicationContext: initialization
compl...

2014-06-11 22:50:26.825 ... : Mapping servlet: 'dispatcherServlet' to [/]

2014-06-11 22:50:26.827 ... : Mapping filter: 'hiddenHttpMethodFilter'
to: [/*]

2014-06-11 22:50:27.332 ... : Mapped URL path [/**/favicon.ico] onto
handler o...

2014-06-11 22:50:27.406 ... : Mapped "{[/],methods=[],params=[],headers=[
],con...

2014-06-11 22:50:27.408 ... : Mapped "{[/error],methods=[],params=[],head
ers=[...

2014-06-11 22:50:27.408 ... : Mapped "{[/error],methods=[],params=[],head
ers=[...

2014-06-11 22:50:27.416 ... : Adding welcome page: file:/Users/
gturnquist/Drop...

2014-06-11 22:50:27.418 ... : Root mapping to handler of type [class org.
sprin...

2014-06-11 22:50:27.429 ... : Mapped URL path [/**] onto handler of type
[clas...

2014-06-11 22:50:27.429 ... : Mapped URL path [/webjars/**] onto handler
of ty...

2014-06-11 22:50:27.968 ... : Registering beans for JMX exposure on
startup

2014-06-11 22:50:27.993 ... : Tomcat started on port(s): 8080/http

2014-06-11 22:50:27.994 ... : Started application in 3.937 seconds (JVM
runnin...
```

 The console output has been edited to better fit this book.

Visit `http://localhost:8080` in a browser to see the following output:

So, what all just happened? Let's walk through each phase.

The `spring` tool parsed `app.groovy` and spotted the `@RestController` annotation. This tipped it off to add Spring MVC to the classpath using Groovy's `@Grab` annotation (`spring` also does this if it spots `@Controller` or `@EnableWebMvc`). It makes our app look like the following code:

```
//@Grab("spring-boot-starter-web")
//@Grab("groovy-templates")

@RestController
class App {
    @RequestMapping("/")
    def home() {
        "Hello, world!"
    }
}
```

Downloading the example code

You can download the example code files for all Packt books you have purchased from your account at `http://www.packtpub.com`. If you purchased this book elsewhere, you can visit `http://www.packtpub.com/support` and register to have the files e-mailed directly to you.

Our preceding code has been manipulated like this:

- The `@Grab` annotation is part of Groovy Grape (`http://groovy.codehaus.org/Grape`), a tool that pulls down third-party libraries from Maven central

- The `spring-boot-starter-web` package is a Spring Boot package that pulls in all the dependencies needed for a Spring MVC app

- The `groovy-templates` package gives us the option to use Groovy's built-in template support (which we aren't using in this example, but is included nonetheless)

Why are the first lines commented out? It's because these lines aren't *really* added to the code we wrote. Spring Boot doesn't use code generation, but instead makes changes inside its embedded Groovy compiler. The comments are simply to clarify what we wrote versus what Spring Boot effectively configured for us.

For those already familiar with Groovy Grape, it's true that `@Grab` actually requires a **group ID**, an **artifact ID**, and a **version**. However, `spring` has a shortcut; if we use a library supported by Spring Boot, we only need to specify the artifact ID. The rest of the library's coordinates are supplied by `spring` and are based on the version of Spring Boot's CLI we have installed. See `https://github.com/spring-projects/spring-boot/blob/v1.1.6.RELEASE/spring-boot-dependencies/pom.xml` for a detailed listing of supported libraries.

After adding these extra libraries, `spring` inserted a few extra import statements, as shown in the following code:

```
//@Grab("spring-boot-starter-web")
//@Grab("groovy-templates")

//import org.springframework.web.bind.annotation.*
//import org.springframework.web.servlet.config.annotation.*
//import org.springframework.web.servlet.*
//import org.springframework.web.servlet.handler.*
//import org.springframework.http.*
//import org.springframework.ui.*

//static import org.springframework.boot.cli.template.GroovyTemplate.
template

@RestController
class App {
    @RequestMapping("/")
    def home() {
        "Hello, world!"
    }
}
```

These particular import statements are for Spring MVC. By automatically supplying these critical import statements, we don't need to know where `@RestController` or `@RequestMapping` are located. We don't need a particular IDE to solve it for us either. Instead, we can focus on the app and not worry about such low-level intimate details of Spring MVC.

Finally, `spring` adds Spring Boot's `@EnableAutoConfiguration` annotation to the class and creates a `static void main` method to run our app, as shown in the following code:

```
//@Grab("spring-boot-starter-web")
//@Grab("groovy-templates")

//import org.springframework.web.bind.annotation.*
//import org.springframework.web.servlet.config.annotation.*
//import org.springframework.web.servlet.*
//import org.springframework.web.servlet.handler.*
//import org.springframework.http.*
//import org.springframework.ui.*

//static import org.springframework.boot.cli.template.GroovyTemplate.
template

//@EnableAutoConfiguration
@RestController
class App {
    @RequestMapping("/")
    def home() {
        "Hello, world!"
    }

    //static void main(String[] args) {
    //    SpringApplication.run(App.class, args)
    //}
}
```

Let's break down this `App` class:

- The `@EnableAutoConfiguration` annotation signals Spring Boot to start making opinionated decisions on adding various components to our app. For example, since Spring MVC was pulled in, many critical beans are created that include view resolvers, an embedded Tomcat servlet container, and a dispatcher servlet. These and other components are created automatically and added to the application context, powering up our app.

- The `SpringApplication.run()` method is Spring Boot's API to start up our app and create an application context. Wrapping it in `static void main` means that we can run this app anywhere there is a JVM installed.

 We can also run `spring run -d app.groovy` to get Spring Boot's auto-configuration report, unveiling the decisions Spring Boot made. For more details about this report, see *Chapter 3, Debugging and Managing Your App.*

In the console output displayed earlier, we not only see the embedded Apache Tomcat servlet container, but also details about Spring MVC being configured. Let's zero in on one line of that console output. The following line shows one Spring MVC route being configured:

```
2014-06-11 22:50:27.406 ... : Mapped "{[/],methods=[],params=[],headers=[
],con...
```

We can see our route to /. Even though it's not visible in this book, running the code will show definite linkage to our `home()` method.

Let's pick another line from that console output to checkout Tomcat's settings. The embedded Tomcat container is configured to run on port `8080`, shown as follows (we'll learn how to easily change this later on in the book):

```
2014-06-11 22:50:27.993 ... : Tomcat started on port(s): 8080/http
```

Have you built Spring MVC apps before? Perhaps you recognize some of these components. It doesn't really matter if you're not familiar with Spring MVC. Spring Boot fired up enough infrastructure to host our web app and allowed us to concentrate our coding efforts on functional features. In this case, the app simply prints a **Hello** greeting on the web page.

Throughout this book, we'll explore how Spring Boot configures components automatically while keeping us in the driver's seat of app development. Also, we'll discover how to override Boot's opinion when needed.

Installing Spring Boot's CLI

One handy way to install things is with the **Groovy enVironment Manager (GVM)** which is found at http://gvmtool.net. It's cross platform and lets you manage multiple versions of various tools from the Groovy community, including Spring Boot's CLI. Installing gvm is super easy with the following command:

```
$ curl -s get.gvmtool.net | bash
```

If you are on Windows, of course, you'll have to visit the website for more directions. Assuming we have gvm installed, this is all it takes to install the Spring Boot CLI:

```
$ gvm install springboot
$ spring --version
Spring CLI v1.1.6.RELEASE
$ gvm ls springboot


================================================================================
Available Springboot Versions
================================================================================
> * 1.1.6.RELEASE
...

================================================================================
+ - local version
* - installed
> - currently in use
================================================================================
```

With GVM, you can readily switch to other versions by typing gvm use springboot <other version>.

There is an alternative if you are using a Mac. One of the most popular package managers for OS X is Homebrew (http://brew.sh). Assuming you have already set up brew, you can install the spring tool by typing:

```
$ brew tap pivotal/tap
$ brew install springboot
$ spring --version
Spring CLI v1.1.6.RELEASE
```

pivotal/tap (https://github.com/pivotal/homebrew-tap) is a Homebrew extension point with many modules from Pivotal, including Spring Boot's CLI tool.

You can also download the bits directly using the following URLs, although one of the preceding solutions is recommended:

- `http://repo.spring.io/release/org/springframework/boot/spring-boot-cli/1.1.6.RELEASE/spring-boot-cli-1.1.6.RELEASE-bin.zip`
- `http://repo.spring.io/release/org/springframework/boot/spring-boot-cli/1.1.6.RELEASE/spring-boot-cli-1.1.6.RELEASE-bin.tar.gz`

Let's check out Spring Boot's CLI commands! To get a listing of what commands are available, use the following argument:

```
$ spring --help
```

We get a listing that includes these commands and common options:

Command	Description
`run [options] <files> [--] [args]`	This runs a Spring Groovy script
`test [options] <files> [--] [args]`	This runs a Spring Groovy script test
`grab`	This downloads a Spring Groovy script's dependencies to `./repository`
`jar [options] <jar-name> <files>`	This creates a self-contained executable JAR file from a Spring Groovy script
`shell`	This starts a nested shell
`-d, --debug Verbose mode`	This prints additional status information for the command you are running

The most commonly used commands are `run`, `test`, and `jar`. We already used `run` at the beginning of this chapter. In the next section, we'll explore how to write some tests and run them with the `test` command. Further on in this chapter, we'll see how to bundle up our code into a runnable JAR file with the `jar` command.

Testing with Spring Boot's CLI

So far, we've seen a tiny app power up using the popular Spring and Apache Tomcat web stack with little effort from our end. Spring Boot was able to detect that we wanted a Spring MVC app, and it put together the components we needed. However, in this day and age, no application is complete without coding some tests. Let's dig in a little more and see how to write some automated tests.

The `spring test` command kicks off Spring Boot; however, instead of magically adding a `static void main` method to run our app, it auto-configures test runners based on the code we supply. Let's first look at this example of a domain class and its related test case found inside Spring Boot's collection of test cases:

```groovy
class Book {
    String author
    String title
}

class BookTests {
    @Test
    void testBooks() {
        Book book = new Book(author: "Tom Clancy",
                                title: "Threat Vector")
        assertEquals("Tom Clancy", book.author)
    }
}
```

The `Book` class is a simple domain object with two fields. The `BookTests` class is a class with a single test method flagged by JUnit's `@Test` annotation.

 This chunk of code is part of Spring Boot's official collection of automated tests at `https://github.com/spring-projects/spring-boot/blob/master/spring-boot-cli/test-samples/book_and_tests.groovy`. In fact, there is a huge collection of samples for various features offered by Spring Boot CLI in the `test-samples` folder.

To run the tests, copy the preceding code into `book_and_tests.groovy` and invoke the `test` command:

```
$ spring test book_and_tests.groovy
Time: 0.264


OK (1 test)
```

Our test case passed! However, no test checkout is complete without a test failure. Let's force it to fail by replacing `assertEquals("Tom Clancy", book.author)` with `assertEquals("Tom Clancy", book.title)`:

```
$ spring test book_and_tests.groovy
.E
Time: 0.262
There was 1 failure:
1) testBooks(BookTests)
org.junit.ComparisonFailure: expected:<T[om Clancy]> but was:<T[hreat
Vector]>
    at org.junit.Assert.assertEquals(Assert.java:115)
    at org.junit.Assert.assertEquals(Assert.java:144)
    at org.junit.Assert$assertEquals.callStatic(Unknown Source)
    ...
    at BookTests.testBooks(book_and_tests.groovy:10)
...
FAILURES!!!
Tests run: 1,  Failures: 1
```

It failed on a string match as expected. Looking down the call stack, we can see exactly where it failed: `book_and_tests.groovy:10`. We changed the **actual** to `book.title` while keeping the **expected** at `Tom Clancy`.

JUnit isn't the only test framework `spring` supports. Spock (`https://code.google.com/p/spock`) is a very popular testing framework in the Groovy community. The `spring test` command supports it as well. An example of the Spoke framework is as follows:

```
class HelloSpock extends Specification {
    def "length of Spock's and his friends' names"() {
        expect:
        name.size() == length

        where:
        name      | length
        "Spock"   | 5
        "Kirk"    | 4
        "Scotty"  | 6
    }
}
```

This code sample is also part of Boot's set of tests at `https://github.com/spring-projects/spring-boot/blob/master/spring-boot-cli/test-samples/spock.groovy`.

This test takes advantage of Groovy's ability to create a method name. By wrapping the string with double quotes, `"length of Spock's and his friends' names"()` becomes a legal method name. This pays off during test failures by providing a comprehensible error message that is also directly tied to the code, as we'll see later.

This test example shows a test closure at the top (`expect: name.size() == length`) followed by a table of inputs. Spock will iterate over each entry in the table and run it through the expect clause as a separate test. This is convenient when we need to run a series of data inputs and their expected outputs through a single test scenario and want to avoid writing multiple method calls.

The `spring` tool spots this code as a test because `HelloSpock` extends Spock's `Specification` interface:

```
$ spring test spock.groovy
.

Time: 0.22


OK (1 test)
```

Again, if we muck up our test case by replacing 4 with 40 and 6 with 16, we can see why it failed and where:

```
$ spring test spock.groovy
.EE
Time: 0.294
There were 2 failures:
1) length of Spock's and his friends' names(HelloSpock)
Condition not satisfied:

name.size() == length
|    |       |  |
Kirk 4       |  40
             false
```

```
    at HelloSpock.length of Spock's and his friends' names(spock.
groovy:4)
2) length of Spock's and his friends' names(HelloSpock)
Condition not satisfied:


name.size() == length
|     |      |   |
|     6      |   16
Scotty      false


    at HelloSpock.length of Spock's and his friends' names(spock.
groovy:4)


FAILURES!!!
Tests run: 1,   Failures: 2
```

This easy-to-read assertion output is thanks to Groovy's power assertions (http://groovy-lang.org/docs/groovy-2.3.0/html/documentation/core-testing-guide.html#_power_assertions) and not restricted to Spock.

> A common issue with running more than one set of inputs and outputs through a single scenario is if the testing framework halts after the first error. With Spock, it clearly runs all inputs and shows us multiple failures, allowing us to fix bugs faster.

It's also easy to run both at the same time. Spring Boot can mix and match testing styles with ease:

```
$ spring test *.groovy
..
Time: 0.288


OK (2 tests)
```

In both our JUnit and Spock test cases, we didn't have to add any @Grab statements to pull in the libraries nor did we need any import statements. The spring test command automatically adds them in for us so we can work on writing the tests.

Which test suite is better, JUnit or Spock? Personally, I have more experience with JUnit, but Spock provides powerful assertion operations, the ability to give readable test names, and a strong way to iterate over multiple sets of data. If I were using Groovy for everyday application development, I would probably migrate towards Spock.

While reducing the need for `@Grab` and import statements reduces the amount of code we need to manage, some IDEs might not be up to date with Spring Boot CLI support, and hence report errors.

Bundling and deploying a Spring Boot application

So far, we have created a web app that fits in a tweet! This is reminiscent of Rob Winch's popular tweet:

Since the time of Rob's famous tweet, the Spring Framework has come out with `@RestController`, an annotation that is basically `@Controller` plus `@ResponseBody`. Using this, the code in this tweet can be reduced down to `@RestController class ThisWillActuallyRun { @RequestMapping("/") String home() { "Hello world!" } }`.

Next, we wrote some super simple automated tests. A big step for any application is deploying it to production. The `spring` tool gives us the means with its `jar` command:

```
$ spring jar app.jar app.groovy
```

This isn't just any JAR file. It's an executable JAR file with all the required dependencies embedded inside it.

I invite you to look inside the JAR file by typing `jar tvf app.jar`. It's not printed here for space reasons, but it contains several key parts:

- Compiled `App.class` based on `app.groovy` is included
- All required libraries are found in the `lib/` folder
- Spring Boot adds a little extra code designed to load and run the nested JAR files

> Java doesn't provide any standardized way to load nested JAR files. Many people have tried to fill this gap by creating "shaded" JARs by unpacking all the class files and repacking them directly into the enclosing JAR file. This makes it hard to spot the libraries, removes their encapsulation, and even has the potential to violate certain project's licensing agreements. Boot instead provides the means to bundle up third-party JARs inside an enclosing JAR file and properly load them at runtime. Read more at `http://docs.spring.io/spring-boot/docs/1.1.6.RELEASE/reference/htmlsingle/#executable-jar`.

With our handy-dandy runnable JAR assembled, there's nothing left to do but run it:

```
$ java -jar app.jar
```

```
  .   ____          _            __ _ _
 /\\ / ___'_ __ _ _(_)_ __  __ _ \ \ \ \
( ( )\___ | '_ | '_| | '_ \/ _` | \ \ \ \
 \\/  ___)| |_)| | | | | || (_| |  ) ) ) )
  '  |____| .__|_| |_|_| |_\__, | / / / /
 =========|_|==============|___/=/_/_/_/
 :: Spring Boot ::        (v1.1.6.RELEASE)


2014-06-11 22:55:54.807 ... : Starting PackagedSpringApplicationLauncher
on re...
2014-06-11 22:55:55.033 ... : Refreshing org.springframework.boot.
context.embe...
```

```
2014-06-11 22:55:55.621 ... : Overriding bean definition for bean
'beanNameVie...
2014-06-11 22:55:56.578 ... : Server initialized with port: 8080
...
```

What are the implications? We can easily take our runnable JAR file and deploy it anywhere there is a JVM:

- If our production environment is on a separate, private network, we can put the JAR file on a flash drive and walk it out to the server room

- If we have SSH access, we can upload it from our development workstation

- If we are using some PaaS provider such as Cloud Foundry (public, private, or hybrid), we can push it by typing `cf push <my app name> -p app.jar`

- We can stage it on our extranet FTP site for customers or other team members to grab a copy

- And…just about any other option imaginable

Even though Oracle officially ended all public updates to Java 6 in February 2013, Spring Boot still supports it. Spring Boot leverages many parts of Spring Framework 4.0 (especially the `@Conditional` annotation), which requires a minimum of Java 6. Java 6 has shown a relatively healthy adoption, so the odds of finding a machine unable to run any apps built with Boot are minuscule. Don't worry if you are using Java 7 or 8; Spring Framework 4 is ready to make full use of this as well!

Spring Boot uses embeddable Tomcat, so there isn't a hard requirement for any type of container to be installed on the target machine. Non-web apps (we'll explore this later in the book) don't even require Apache Tomcat. The JAR file itself is the new container that allows us to stop thinking in terms of old fashioned servlet containers. Instead, we can think in terms of apps. All these factors add up to maximum flexibility in application deployment.

Adding support for templates

Okay, we've created a super simple application using Groovy and Spring Boot. We also bundled it up as a runnable JAR file that can be deployed anywhere we can find a Java 6 (or higher) JVM. However, this toy app we've built so far was hard coded with **Hello, world!** content. Real apps need views that can handle dynamic data, right? Let's make some tweaks and call it `app_with_views.groovy`, as shown in the following code:

```
@Grab("thymeleaf-spring4")
@Controller
```

```
class ViewBasedApp {

    def chapters = ["Quick Start With Groovy",
        "Quick Start With Java",
        "Debugging and Managing Your App",
        "Data Access with Spring Boot",
        "Securing Your App"]

    @RequestMapping("/")
    def home (@RequestParam(value="name", defaultValue="World")
    String n) {
        new ModelAndView("home")
            .addObject("name", n)
            .addObject("chapters", chapters)
    }
}
```

What did we just do? We can see the following listed here:

- The `@Grab("thymeleaf-spring4")` annotation pulls in the Thymeleaf template engine, which causes Boot to auto-configure some more infrastructure. Boot supports several template engines, but we'll be using Thymeleaf throughout this book.

- Replacing `@RestController` with `@Controller` indicates that the return value of route methods is a view and not raw content.

- The `@RequestParam` annotation lets us grab the incoming `name` parameter and put it in the view's `ModelAndView` instance.

- The `ModelAndView` class is a nice container that lets us specify the view name and provide data objects to whatever template engine we choose (Thymeleaf in this case).

- We are also using a fixed list of chapter titles from this book as additional data for the page to render. This simulates content being fetched from a database.

 While this book uses Thymeleaf, Spring MVC doesn't require a particular template engine in order to use its model and view classes.

We need to craft our `home` template. Spring Boot auto-configures settings for multiple engines. When it comes to Thymeleaf, it prefixes all view names with `templates/` and appends `.html` at the end. (See `http://docs.spring.io/spring-boot/docs/1.1.6.RELEASE/reference/htmlsingle/#boot-features-spring-mvc-template-engines` for more information.) To do so, we first need to create the `templates` directory adjacent to our code. Otherwise, Spring Boot CLI won't be able to find our template. Next, let's create `templates/home.html`, as shown in the following code:

```html
<html>
    <head>
        <title>Learning Spring Boot - Chapter 1</title>
    </head>
    <body>
        <p th:text="'Hello, ' + ${name}"></p>
        <ol>
            <li th:each="chapter : ${chapters}"
            th:text="${chapter}"></li>
        </ol>
    </body>
</html>
```

Let's break down this template:

- Thymeleaf is HTML compliant, meaning the templates are visible inside a browser without breaking anything (compared to things like JSPs in certain situations). Its engine plugs in via the `th` namespace, using that as the way to introduce expressions, access model objects, and so on.

- The `th:text="'Hello, ' + ${name}"` attribute embedded inside the `<p>` element configures the `text` value of this element. In this case, it concatenates `Hello` with the `name` attribute that was supplied by the server.

- This template also shows a numbered list of chapter titles from this book, using Thymeleaf's `th:each` iterator. Thymeleaf creates one `<li>` tag for each chapter supplied in `ModelAndView` and proceeds to set the `text` value of each line item with that particular row's chapter name.

Let's launch this template-based version of our app:

```
$ spring run app_with_views.groovy
```

If we navigate to the same `http://localhost:8080` as before, we'll see the familiar **Hello, world!**, now accompanied by the listing of chapters. However, if we go to `http://localhost:8080?name=Alice`, we'll instead see **Hello, Alice**, as shown in the following screenshot:

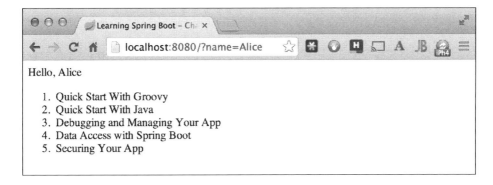

 Thymeleaf has a DOM-based parsing engine. Everything is handled by attributes in the th namespace. This means we can open up a Thymeleaf template with any browser with no problem because it's 100 percent valid HTML. Even though it's the chosen view technology for this book, diving into all of its intricacies would take up too much room. For more details, see http://www.thymeleaf.org.

Modernizing our app with JavaScript

We just saw that, with a single @Grab statement, Spring Boot automatically configured the Thymeleaf template engine and some specialized view resolvers. We took advantage of Spring MVC's ability to pass attributes to the template through ModelAndView. Instead of figuring out the details of view resolvers, we instead channeled our efforts into building a handy template to render data fetched from the server. We didn't have to dig through reference docs, Google, and Stack Overflow to figure out how to configure and integrate Spring MVC with Thymeleaf. We let Spring Boot do the heavy lifting.

But that's not enough, right? Any real application is going to also have some JavaScript. Love it or hate it, JavaScript is the engine for frontend web development. See how the following code lets us make things more modern by creating modern. groovy:

```
@Grab("org.webjars:jquery:2.1.1")
@Grab("thymeleaf-spring4")
@Controller
class ModernApp {

    def chapters = ["Quick Start With Groovy",
        "Quick Start With Java",
        "Debugging and Managing Your App",
```

```
        "Data Access with Spring Boot",
        "Securing Your App"]

    @RequestMapping("/")
    def home(@RequestParam(value="name", defaultValue="World")
    String n) {
        new ModelAndView("modern")
            .addObject("name", n)
            .addObject("chapters", chapters)
    }
}
```

A single `@Grab` statement pulls in jQuery 2.1.1. The rest of our server-side Groovy code is the same as before.

There are multiple ways to use JavaScript libraries. For Java developers, it's especially convenient to use the WebJars project (`http://webjars.org`), where lots of handy JavaScript libraries are wrapped up with Maven coordinates. Every library is found on the `/webjars/<library>/<version>/<module>` path. To top it off, Spring Boot comes with prebuilt support. Perhaps you noticed this buried in earlier console outputs:

```
...

2014-05-20 08:33:09.062  ... : Mapped URL path [/webjars/**] onto handler
of [...

...
```

With jQuery added to our application, we can amp up our template (`templates/ modern.html`) like this:

```html
<html>
    <head>
        <title>Learning Spring Boot - Chapter 1</title>
        <script src="webjars/jquery/2.1.1/jquery.min.js"></script>
        <script>
            $(document).ready(function() {
                $('p').animate({
                    fontSize: '48px',
                }, "slow");
            });
        </script>
    </head>
    <body>
        <p th:text="'Hello, ' + ${name}"></p>
        <ol>
```

```
        <li th:each="chapter : ${chapters}"
        th:text="${chapter}"></li>
    </ol>
  </body>
</html>
```

What's different between this template and the previous one?

It has a couple extra `<script>` tags in the `head` section:

- The first one loads jQuery from `/webjars/jquery/2.1.1/jquery.min.js` (implying that we can also grab `jquery.js` if we want to debug jQuery)

- The second script looks for the `<p>` element containing our **Hello, world!** message and then performs an animation that increases the font size to 48 pixels after the DOM is fully loaded into the browser

If we run `spring run modern.groovy` and visit `http://localhost:8080`, then we can see this simple but stylish animation (which naturally doesn't render as well in a printed book). It shows us that all of jQuery is available for us to work with on our application.

Using Bower instead of WebJars

WebJars isn't the only option when it comes to adding JavaScript to our app. More sophisticated UI developers might use Bower (`http://bower.io`), a popular JavaScript library management tool. WebJars are useful for Java developers, but not every library has been bundled as a WebJar. There is also a huge community of frontend developers more familiar with Bower and NodeJS that will probably prefer using their standard tool chain to do their jobs.

We'll see how to plug that into our app. First, it's important to know some basic options. Spring Boot supports serving up static web resources from the following paths:

- `/META-INF/resources/`
- `/resources/`
- `/static/`
- `/public/`

To craft a Bower-based app with Spring Boot, we first need to craft a `.bowerrc` file in the same folder we plan to create our Spring Boot CLI application. Let's pick `public/` as the folder of choice for JavaScript modules and put it in this file, as shown in the following code:

```
{
    "directory": "public/"
}
```

 Do I have to use `public`? No. Again, you can pick any of the folders listed previously and Spring Boot will serve up the code. It's a matter of taste and semantics.

Our first step towards a Bower-based app is to define our project by answering a series of questions (this only has to be done once):

```
$ bower init
[?] name: app_with_bower
[?] version: 0.1.0
[?] description: Learning Spring Boot - bower sample
[?] main file:
[?] what types of modules does this package expose? amd
[?] keywords:
[?] authors: Greg Turnquist <gturnquist@pivotal.io>
[?] license: ASL
[?] homepage: http://blog.greglturnquist.com/category/learning-spring-
boot
[?] set currently installed components as dependencies? No
[?] add commonly ignored files to ignore list? Yes
[?] would you like to mark this package as private which prevents it from
being accidentally published to the registry? Yes

...

[?] Looks good? Yes
```

Now that we have set our project, let's do something simple such as install jQuery with the following command:

```
$ bower install jquery --save
bower jquery#*                    cached git://github.com/jquery/jquery.
git#2.1.1
bower jquery#*                    validate 2.1.1 against git://github.com/
jquery/jquery.git#*
```

These two commands will have created the following bower.json file:

```json
{
  "name": "app_with_bower",
  "version": "0.1.0",
  "authors": [
    "Greg Turnquist <gturnquist@pivotal.io>"
  ],
  "description": "Learning Spring Boot - bower sample",
  "license": "ASL",
  "homepage": "http://blog.greglturnquist.com/category/learning-
spring-boot",
  "private": true,
  "ignore": [
    "**/.*",
    "node_modules",
    "bower_components",
    "public/",
    "test",
    "tests"
  ],
  "dependencies": {
    "jquery": "~2.1.1"
  }
}
```

It will also have installed jQuery 2.1.1 into our app with the following directory structure:

```
public
└── jquery
    ├── MIT-LICENSE.txt
    ├── bower.json
    └── dist
        ├── jquery.js
        └── jquery.min.js
```

 We must include --save (two dashes) whenever we install a module. This ensures that our bower.json file is updated at the same time, allowing us to rebuild things if needed.

The altered version of our app with WebJars removed should now look like this:

```
@Grab("thymeleaf-spring4")
@Controller
class ModernApp {

    def chapters = ["Quick Start With Groovy",
        "Quick Start With Java",
        "Debugging and Managing Your App",
        "Data Access with Spring Boot",
        "Securing Your App"]

    @RequestMapping("/")
    def home(@RequestParam(value="name", defaultValue="World")
    String n) {
        new ModelAndView("modern_with_bower")
            .addObject("name", n)
            .addObject("chapters", chapters)
    }
}
```

The view name has been changed to modern_with_bower, so it doesn't collide with the previous template if found in the same folder.

This version of the template, templates/modern_with_bower.html, should look like this:

```
<html>
    <head>
        <title>Learning Spring Boot - Chapter 1</title>
        <script src="jquery/dist/jquery.min.js"></script>
        <script>
            $(document).ready(function() {
                $('p').animate({
                    fontSize: '48px',
                }, "slow");
            });
        </script>
    </head>
    <body>
        <p th:text="'Hello, ' + ${name}"></p>
        <ol>
            <li th:each="chapter : ${chapters}"
            th:text="${chapter}"></li>
        </ol>
    </body>
</html>
```

The path to `jquery` is now `jquery/dist/jquery.min.js`. The rest is the same as the WebJars example. We just launch the app with `spring run modern_with_bower.groovy` and navigate to `http://localhost:8080`. (Might need to refresh the page to ensure loading of the latest HTML.) The animation should work just the same.

The options shown in this section can quickly give us a taste of how easy it is to use popular JavaScript tools with Spring Boot. We don't have to fiddle with messy tool chains to achieve a smooth integration. Instead, we can use them the way they are meant to be used.

What about an app that is all frontend with no backend?

Perhaps we're building an app that gets all its data from a remote backend. In this age of RESTful backends, it's not uncommon to build a single page frontend that is fed data updates via AJAX.

Spring Boot's Groovy support provides the perfect and arguably smallest way to get started. We do so by creating `pure_javascript.groovy`, as shown in the following code:

```
@Controller
class JsApp { }
```

That doesn't look like much, but it accomplishes a lot. Let's see what this tiny fragment of code actually does for us:

- The `@Controller` annotation, like `@RestController`, causes Spring Boot to auto-configure Spring MVC.

- Spring Boot, as we've seen throughout this chapter, will launch an embedded Apache Tomcat server.

- Spring Boot will serve up static content from `resources`, `static`, and `public`. Since there are no Spring MVC routes in this tiny fragment of code, things will fall to resource resolution.

Next, we can create a `static/index.html` page as follows:

```
<html>
    Greetings from pure HTML which can, in turn, load JavaScript!
</html>
```

Run `spring run pure_javascript.groovy` and navigate to
`http://localhost:8080`. We will see the preceding plain text shown in
our browser as expected. There is nothing here but pure HTML being served
up by our embedded Apache Tomcat server. This is arguably the lightest way to
serve up static content. Use `spring jar`, as we saw earlier in this chapter, and it's
possible to easily bundle up our client-side app to be installed anywhere.

Spring Boot's support for static HTML, JavaScript, and CSS opens the door to
many options. We can add WebJar annotations to JsApp or use Bower to introduce
third-party JavaScript libraries in addition to any custom client-side code. We might
just manually download the JavaScript and CSS. No matter what option we choose,
Spring Boot CLI certainly provides a super simple way to add rich-client power
for app development. To top it off, RESTful backends that are decoupled from the
frontend can have different iteration cycles as well as different development teams.

 You might need to configure CORS (`http://spring.io/`
`understanding/CORS`) to properly handle making remote
calls that don't go back to the original server.

Adding production-ready support features

So far, we have created a Spring MVC app with minimal code. We added views and
JavaScript. We are on the verge of a production release.

Before deploying our rapidly built and modernized web application, we might want
to think about potential issues that might arise in production:

- What do we do when the system administrator wants to configure his
  monitoring software to ping our app to see if it's up?

- What happens when our manager wants to know the metrics of people
  hitting our app?

- What are we going to do when the Ops center supervisor calls us at 2:00 a.m.
  and we have to figure out what went wrong?

The last feature we are going to introduce in this chapter is Spring Boot's Actuator
module and CRaSH remote shell support (`http://www.crashub.org`). These two
modules provide some super slick, Ops-oriented features that are incredibly valuable
in a production environment.

We first need to update our previous code (we'll call it ops.groovy), as shown in the following code:

```
@Grab("spring-boot-actuator")
@Grab("spring-boot-starter-remote-shell")
@Grab("org.webjars:jquery:2.1.1")
@Grab("thymeleaf-spring4")
@Controller
class OpsReadyApp {
    @RequestMapping("/")
    def home(@RequestParam(value="name", defaultValue="World")
    String n) {
        new ModelAndView("modern")
            .addObject("name", n)
    }
}
```

This app is exactly like the WebJars example with two key differences: it adds @Grab("spring-boot-actuator") and @Grab("spring-boot-starter-remote-shell").

When you run this version of our app, the same business functionality is available that we saw earlier, but there are additional HTTP endpoints available:

Actuator endpoint	Description
/autoconfig	This reports what Spring Boot did and didn't auto-configure and why
/beans	This reports all the beans configured in the application context (including ours as well as the ones auto-configured by Boot)
/configprops	This exposes all configuration properties
/dump	This creates a thread dump report
/env	This reports on the current system environment
/health	This is a simple endpoint to check life of the app
/info	This serves up custom content from the app
/metrics	This shows counters and gauges on web usage
/mappings	This gives us details about all Spring MVC routes
/trace	This shows details about past requests

Pinging our app for general health

Each of these endpoints can be visited using our browser or using other tools such as curl. For example, let's assume we ran spring run `ops.groovy` and then opened up another shell. From the second shell, let's run the following curl command:

```
$ curl localhost:8080/health
{"status":"UP"}
```

This immediately solves our first need listed previously. We can inform the system administrator that he or she can write a management script to interrogate our app's health.

Gathering metrics

Be warned that each of these endpoints serves up a compact JSON document. Generally speaking, command-line curl probably isn't the best option. While it's convenient on *nix and Mac systems, the content is dense and hard to read. It's more practical to have:

- A JSON plugin installed in our browser (such as JSONView at `http://jsonview.com`)

- A script that uses a JSON parsing library if we're writing a management script (such as Groovy's JsonSlurper at `http://groovy.codehaus.org/gapi/groovy/json/JsonSlurper.html` or JSONPath at `https://code.google.com/p/json-path`)

Assuming we have JSONView installed, the following screenshot shows a listing of metrics:

It lists **counters** for each HTTP endpoint. According to this, /metrics has been visited four times with a successful 200 status code. Someone tried to access /foo, but it failed with a 404 error code. The report also lists **gauges** for each endpoint, reporting the last response time. In this case, /metrics took 2 milliseconds. Also included are some memory stats as well as the total CPUs available.

> It's important to realize that the metrics start at 0. To generate some numbers, you might want to first click on some links before visiting /metrics.

The following screenshot shows a trace report:

```
[
  - {
      timestamp: 1400731322578,
      - info: {
          method: "GET",
          path: "/health",
          - headers: {
              - request: {
                  user-agent: "curl/7.30.0",
                  host: "localhost:8080",
                  accept: "*/*"
                },
              - response: {
                  X-Application-Context: "application",
                  Content-Type: "text/plain;charset=ISO-8859-1",
                  Content-Length: "2",
                  Date: "Thu, 22 May 2014 04:02:02 GMT",
                  status: "200"
                }
            }
        }
    },
  - {
      timestamp: 1400731336947,
      - info: {
          method: "GET",
```

It shows the entire web request and response for curl localhost:8080/health.

This provides a basic framework of metrics to satisfy our manager's needs. It's important to understand that metrics gathered by Spring Boot Actuator aren't persistent across application restarts. So to gather long-term data, we have to gather them and then write them elsewhere.

With these options, we can perform the following:

- Write a script that gathers metrics every hour and appends them to a running spreadsheet somewhere else in the filesystem, such as a shared drive. This might be simple, but probably also crude.

- To step it up, we can dump the data into a Hadoop filesystem for raw collection and configure Spring XD (`http://projects.spring.io/spring-xd/`) to consume it. Spring XD stands for **Spring eXtreme Data**. It is an open source product that makes it incredibly easy to chain together sources and sinks comprised of many components, such as HTTP endpoints, Hadoop filesystems, Redis metrics, and RabbitMQ messaging. Unfortunately, there is no space to dive into this subject.

> With any monitoring, it's important to check that we aren't taxing the system too heavily. The same container responding to business-related web requests is also serving metrics data, so it will be wise to engage profilers periodically to ensure that the whole system is performing as expected.

Detailed management with CRaSH

So what can we do when we receive that 2:00 a.m. phone call from the Ops center? After either coming in or logging in remotely, we can access the convenient CRaSH shell we configured.

Every time the app launches, it generates a random password for SSH access and prints this to the local console:

```
2014-06-11 23:00:18.822 ... : Configuring property ssh.port=2000 from
properties

2014-06-11 23:00:18.823 ... : Configuring property ssh.auth-
timeout=600000 fro...

2014-06-11 23:00:18.824 ... : Configuring property ssh.idle-
timeout=600000 fro...

2014-06-11 23:00:18.824 ... : Configuring property auth=simple from
properties

2014-06-11 23:00:18.824 ... : Configuring property auth.simple.
username=user f...

2014-06-11 23:00:18.824 ... : Configuring property auth.simple.
password=bdbe4a...
```

We can easily see that there's SSH access on port 2000 via a user if we use this information to log in:

```
$ ssh -p 2000 user@localhost
Password authentication
Password:
```

```
  .   ____
 /\\ / ___'_ __ _ _(_)_ __  __ _ \ \ \ \
( ( )\___ | '_ | '_| | '_ \/ _` | \ \ \ \
 \\/  ___)| |_)| | | | | || (_| |  ) ) ) )
  '  |____| .__|_| |_|_| |_\__, | / / / /
 =========|_|==============|___/=/_/_/_/
 :: Spring Boot ::   (v1.1.6.RELEASE) on retina
>
```

There's a fistful of commands:

- `help`: This gets a listing of available commands
- `dashboard`: This gets a graphic, text-based display of all the threads, environment properties, memory, and other things
- `autoconfig`: This prints out a report of which Spring Boot auto-configuration rules were applied and which were skipped (and why)

All of the previous commands have man pages:

```
> man autoconfig
NAME
        autoconfig - Display auto configuration report from
ApplicationContext


SYNOPSIS
        autoconfig [-h | --help]


STREAM
        autoconfig <java.lang.Void, java.lang.Object>


PARAMETERS
        [-h | --help]
            Display this help message
...
```

There are many commands available to help manage our application. More details are available at http://www.crashub.org/1.3/reference.html.

This is just a taste of what's possible. Later on in *Chapter 2, Quick Start with Java*, and *Chapter 3, Debugging and Managing Your App*, we will dig in deeper to discover ways to write custom metrics, custom health checks, and custom CRaSH commands.

Summary

We rapidly crafted a Spring MVC application using the Spring stack on top of Apache Tomcat with little configuration from our end. We plugged in jQuery (and could have included CSS if we wanted). We also learned how to write both JUnit and Spock test cases. We plugged in Spring Boot's Actuator module as well as the CRaSH remote shell, configuring it with metrics, health, and management features so that we can monitor it in production by merely adding two lines of extra code.

In the next chapter, we'll do something quite similar, but with pure Java and a sample application that focuses on fetching GitHub information.

2
Quick Start with Java

"With Boot you deploy everywhere you can find a JVM basically."

– Oliver Gierke `@olivergierke`

In the previous chapter, we saw how quickly an application can be created with just a few lines of code. To fit the more commonly used paradigm, this chapter (and the rest of the book) will use a project with a build file and Java code instead. However, we'll still see how Spring Boot makes things quick and easy.

In this chapter, we are going to build an app that scans GitHub issues and uses Spring Boot to help guide us in reducing the complexity of integrating multiple Spring projects as well as other third-party libraries.

In this chapter, we will be:

- Using `http://start.spring.io` to create a bare bones Spring Boot project with Gradle support
- Creating a simple app that looks for open issues in multiple GitHub repositories
- Supplying GitHub credentials using Boot's über easy property support
- Learning how Boot finds templates
- Adding mobile support using Spring Mobile and jQuery Mobile
- Bundling up the application as a runnable JAR and deploying it to Cloud Foundry
- Adding production-ready support with Actuator and then writing a script to poll for usage metrics

Creating an empty project with start.spring.io

To kick things off, we need a new project. Instead of starting from absolutely nothing, Spring Boot provides a website that is used to create new projects at `http://start.spring.io`. We enter some information, pick a set of desired options, and then download either a build file or a zipped-up project.

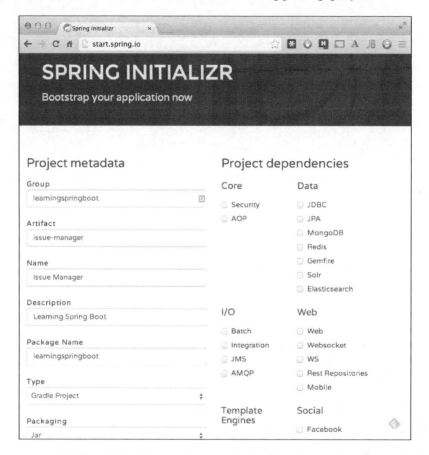

The screen is a bit long and was cut off. The following table shows you all the settings filled in for this example. However, to see the code behind this website, visit `https://github.com/spring-io/initializr`. To whet your appetite, the site is, in fact, a Spring Boot / Groovy app using the same tools covered in the previous chapter.

As shown in the previous screenshot, we entered this information:

Field	Value
Group	`learningspringboot`
Artifact	`issue-manager`
Name	`Issue Manager`
Description	`Learning Spring Boot`
Package Name	`learningspringboot`
Type	**Gradle Project**
Packaging	**Jar**
Java Version	**1.8**
Language	**Java**
Project dependencies	**Thymeleaf**

Click on the **Generate Project** button; it downloads `starter.zip`. Let's take a peek inside the ZIP file:

```
$ unzip -l <downloaded zip file>
Archive:  starter.zip
Length      Date    Time      Name
--------    ----    ----      ----
      0   06-13-14 03:37    src/
      0   06-13-14 03:37    src/main/
      0   06-13-14 03:37    src/main/java/
      0   06-13-14 03:37    src/main/java/learningspringboot/
      0   06-13-14 03:37    src/main/resources/
      0   06-13-14 03:37    src/test/
      0   06-13-14 03:37    src/test/java/
      0   06-13-14 03:37    src/test/java/learningspringboot/
   1421   06-13-14 03:37     build.gradle
    466   06-13-14 03:37    src/main/java/learningspringboot/Application.
java
      0   06-13-14 03:37    src/main/resources/application.properties
    404   06-13-14 03:37    src/test/java/learningspringboot/
ApplicationTests.java
--------                    -------
   2291                     12 files
```

Let's take a look at what we have:

- A standard Gradle project layout (`src/main/java`, `src/main/resources`, `src/test/java`, and `src/test/resources`)
- The root Java package, which is `learningspringboot`
- A `build.gradle` file, which we'll look at later in this chapter
- A couple of classes that are already created: `Application.java` and `ApplicationTests.java`
- A properties file (`application.properties`) that we'll discuss in the next section

 Feel free to pick to pick the build system you want. Spring Boot has equivalent support for Maven. It's also possible to use Ant, but Spring Boot has no special support for it. For reasons of space and other factors, this book will focus on Gradle and not show apps expressed in any other build system.

Before looking at the generated code, let's look at the build file:

```
// tag::plugins[]
buildscript {
    repositories {
        mavenCentral()
    }
    dependencies {
        classpath("org.springframework.boot:spring-boot-gradle-
            plugin:1.1.6.RELEASE")
    }
}
// end::plugins[]

apply plugin: 'java'
apply plugin: 'eclipse'
apply plugin: 'idea'
apply plugin: 'spring-boot'

jar {
    baseName = 'issue-manager'
    version = '0.0.1-SNAPSHOT'
}

// tag::version[]
sourceCompatibility = 1.8
```

```
targetCompatibility = 1.8
// end::version[]

repositories {
    mavenCentral()
}


// tag::dependencies[]
dependencies {
    compile("org.springframework.boot:spring-boot-starter-
        thymeleaf")
    testCompile("org.springframework.boot:spring-boot-starter-
        test")
}
// end::dependencies[]

task wrapper(type: Wrapper) {
    gradleVersion = '2.1'
}
```

There are a quite a few parts to this file, so let's walk through them bit by bit.

 You might see some comments such as `<!-- tag::x-y-z[] -->` in `build.gradle` and other files throughout this book. These are simple comments that are used to help pull in subsections for more detailed explanations and are *not* required to run any code you write.

The first important nugget at the top is this:

```
buildscript {
    repositories {
        mavenCentral()
    }
    dependencies {
        classpath("org.springframework.boot:spring-boot-gradle-
            plugin:1.1.6.RELEASE")
    }
}
```

This shows you our project, which is configured to pull down packages from `mavenCentral`. However, more importantly, our package is using `spring-boot-gradle-plugin`, Version 1.1.6.RELEASE. A key feature that we will see in this chapter and through the rest of this book is Spring Boot's series of predefined versions for many third-party libraries (not just Spring projects). By using this plugin, Spring Boot will set the version number for any dependency we declare that it happens to manage.

Continuing to check out our build file, we can see a list of dependencies:

```
dependencies {
    compile("org.springframework.boot:spring-boot-starter-
        thymeleaf")
    testCompile("org.springframework.boot:spring-boot-starter-
        test")
}
```

These include the following:

- `spring-boot-starter-thymeleaf`: This pulls in dependencies that are required in order to use Thymeleaf as our view engine
- `spring-boot-starter-test`: This pulls in Spring test utilities when we are running tests

The first one matches the checkbox we picked on the form (but couldn't see directly due to the cutoff): **Thymeleaf**. The second one is included in all projects, given the popularity of automated testing in this day and age.

So, what are these quirky packages? They definitely look different than any packages we might have used in the past, which we will find out about in the next section. Before we do that, let's look at another key setting:

```
sourceCompatibility = 1.8
targetCompatibility = 1.8
```

This specifies that the project is using Java 8. While Spring Boot provides support as far back as Java 6, we plan to take advantage of the latest features that are out there throughout this book.

Spring Boot starters

The packages that were plugged in by `start.spring.io` are known as **Spring Boot starters**. They are virtual packages that are deployed to Maven central. Their job is to pull in other dependencies while containing no code of their own.

To go into more detail about starters, let's pick this one: `spring-boot-starter-thymeleaf`. If we look at its `pom.xml` build file online (`https://github.com/spring-projects/spring-boot/tree/v1.1.6.RELEASE/spring-boot-starters/spring-boot-starter-thymeleaf/pom.xml`), we will see the following dependencies:

Dependency	What it provides
`spring-boot-starter`	A starter that brings in core dependencies that are critical for any Spring Boot-based project
`spring-boot-starter-web`	A starter that brings in embedded Tomcat, Jackson JSON binding, JSR 303 validation APIs, and Spring Web plus MVC support
`spring-core`	Critical parts of the Spring Framework (`http://projects.spring.io/spring-framework`)
`thymeleaf-spring4`	Core pieces of the Thymeleaf view engine along with Spring 4 integration
`thymeleaf-layout-dialect`	Thymeleaf dialect module

 Wait, I thought this book was focused on Gradle! That's true, but Spring Boot itself is built with Maven. It is valuable to look at any of Spring Boot's starters in order to glean what they do.

Spring Boot is designed to help us build good apps rapidly. A key piece of making this happen is how Boot plugs in its opinion. When we include `spring-boot-starter-thymeleaf`, Spring Boot has the opinion that we'll probably want embedded Tomcat, Jackson JSON support, JSR 303 validation, and Spring Web MVC. So, it adds them as required dependencies.

Notice how there are no version numbers in the `dependencies` section? This is because each dependency we see listed is preset with a version number supplied by `spring-boot-gradle-plugin`. It's another opinion from Spring Boot about the best version of the library to use in conjunction with all the others.

The last thing Boot does is make auto-configuration decisions. The previous chapter showed us many examples of this, and it's happening here as well. Spring Boot configured view resolvers, an embedded servlet container, and other components that are commonly recommended for Spring MVC apps.

As we continue along this chapter, and throughout this book, we'll get to see more opinions that Boot inserts (and how it backs off when we make a different decision).

 This amalgamation of libraries and chosen versions is known as **Spring IO** (http://spring.io/platform) and offers an out-of-the-box virtual collection of libraries that are verified to work together. Spring IO is very easy to use, as it's served up through the industry-standard Maven public repositories; it's not a downloadable bundle that becomes outdated the day after you get it.

Running a Spring Boot application

So far, we have a bare bones project. There isn't much code. However, http://start.spring.io creates a single Application class; let's look at that first:

```java
package learningspringboot;

import org.springframework.boot.SpringApplication;
import org.springframework.boot.autoconfigure.EnableAutoConfiguration;
import org.springframework.context.annotation.ComponentScan;

@ComponentScan
@EnableAutoConfiguration
public class Application {

    public static void main(String[] args) {
        SpringApplication.run(Application.class, args);
    }
}
```

Let's break this down:

- @ComponentScan: This tells Spring to look for classes with @Component, @Configuration, @Repository, @Service, and @Controller and wire them into the app context as beans. By default, it scans for classes found underneath the package where the annotation is declared.

- @EnableAutoConfiguration: This turns on Boot's auto-configuration behavior.

- public static void main(): This uses Boot's SpringApplication.run() method as a convenient way to launch the app.

The `@EnableAutoConfiguration` key annotation is used for a Spring Boot-based application. It tells Boot to turn on all auto-configuration options. Each of these options looks at various aspects of the application and then makes decisions on adding extra beans. It makes decisions mostly based on the classpath and settings found inside `application.properties`.

 Consider this example of auto-configuration. If Boot spots `JmsTemplate.class` on the classpath, it's an indication that the developer has added **spring-jms**. In this situation, Boot will automatically create an instance of `JmsTemplate` and make it available for injection to other Spring beans. The developer must still provide a `ConnectionFactory` bean. More details on how this works can be found in *Chapter 3, Debugging and Managing Your App*, where we will use `JmsAutoConfiguration` as an example.

Spring Boot's `SpringApplication.run()` method conveniently accepts a class as well as command-line arguments. In this case, it's plugging in the `Application` class, as this is the simplest way to build an app. We can start adding bean definitions right here or branch off in other places.

Adding Spring Social GitHub

We have discussed building an app that can scan GitHub repositories for open issues. The first step is to add a key project, which is **Spring Social GitHub**:

1. First, we need to visit `http://projects.spring.io/spring-social-github`.

2. From there, we can scroll down and find the latest release. In this case, we are using `1.0.0.BUILD-SNAPSHOT`, as M4 has some outstanding issues.

3. There's a slider that lets us pick our build system and shows us the content that we need to insert into our project's dependencies:

```
compile("org.springframework.social:spring-social-
github:1.0.0.BUILD-SNAPSHOT")
```

4. This dependency will load Spring Social GitHub. Since it's not a general release, we need to add this to the `repositories` section:

```
repositories {
    mavenCentral()
    maven { url "https://repo.spring.io/libs-snapshot" }
}
```

By default, start.spring.io will include mavenCentral in the repositories section. In order to access Spring Social GitHub's BUILD-SNAPSHOT version, we had to add the second Maven URL.

With these two bits added to our build file, we are ready to build our app!

Digging into GitHub issues

Let's continue working on our simple app that will fetch GitHub issues from multiple repositories. To fetch GitHub issues, we need to establish a domain object:

```
package learningspringboot;

import org.springframework.social.github.api.GitHubIssue;

public class Issue {

    private String repo;
    private GitHubIssue githubIssue;

    public Issue(String repo, GitHubIssue gitHubIssue) {
        this.repo = repo;
        this.githubIssue = gitHubIssue;
    }

    public String getRepo() {
        return repo;
    }

    public GitHubIssue getGithubIssue() {
        return githubIssue;
    }
}
```

Spring Social GitHub comes with a GitHubIssue class, but this class doesn't include the name of the repository for a given issue. The Issue class listed in the preceding code is basically a wrapper that adds this extra bit of information. It's designed to be created through a constructor call that minimizes the risk of initializing it incompletely. It also includes getter calls in order to retrieve the data fields.

Next, we need a service that uses Spring Social GitHub's `GitHubTemplate` to retrieve issues:

```
package learningspringboot;

import java.util.ArrayList;
import java.util.List;

import org.springframework.social.github.api.GitHubIssue;
import org.springframework.social.github.api.impl.GitHubTemplate;
import org.springframework.stereotype.Service;

@Service
public class IssueManager {

    String githubToken =
        "ccdbf257f052a594a0e7bd2823a69ae38a48ffb1";

    String org = "spring-projects";

    String[] repos = new String[] { "spring-boot", "spring-boot-
        issues" };

    GitHubTemplate gitHubTemplate = new
        GitHubTemplate(githubToken);

    public List<Issue> findOpenIssues() {
        List<Issue> openIssues = new ArrayList<>();

        for (String repo : repos) {
            final List<GitHubIssue> issues = gitHubTemplate
                .repoOperations().getIssues(org, repo);

            for (GitHubIssue issue : issues) {
                if (issue.getState().equals("open")) {
                    openIssues.add(new Issue(repo, issue));
                }
            }
        }

        return openIssues;

    }
}
```

This class is marked as `@Service`, which means that it will be picked up and added to the app context by `@ComponentScan`. All of Spring's component annotations inherit from `@Component`, which gets them picked up by component scanning. It has a hardcoded GitHub passcode and a hardcoded organization name, and will fetch issues from spring-boot and spring-boot-issues. This service also has a `GitHubTemplate`.

The key function of this class, which is `findOpenIssues`, loops through the list of repositories, and then uses `GitHubTemplate` to retrieve open issues. It gathers them into a standard list, wrapped inside the `Issue` object we coded earlier.

Creating a GitHub access token

From where did we get this cryptic `githubToken` value of `ccdbf257f052a594a0e7bd2823a69ae38a48ffb1`? This is an `oauth` access code that is required to plug in and talk to GitHub. To create one of your own, you need to create an account at `https://github.com`. After creating your account, perform the following steps:

1. Assuming the account is set up, visit `https://github.com/settings/applications`.

2. Scroll down until you see **Personal access tokens**.

3. Click on **Generate new token**. You'll probably be prompted to confirm your password.

4. Enter a description such as `Learning Spring Boot`, accept the default access controls, and click on **Generate token**.

You'll now see a newly minted cryptic token code with a copy-to-clipboard icon to the right. Grab it and paste it into your code, and you're ready! Have a look at the following screenshot:

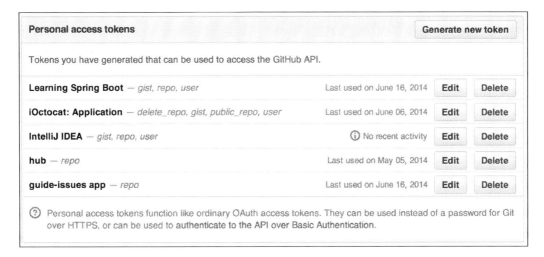

Personal access tokens		**Generate new token**
Tokens you have generated that can be used to access the GitHub API.		

Learning Spring Boot — *gist, repo, user* — Last used on June 16, 2014 — **Edit** **Delete**

iOctocat: Application — *delete_repo, gist, public_repo, user* — Last used on June 06, 2014 — **Edit** **Delete**

IntelliJ IDEA — *gist, repo, user* — ⓘ No recent activity — **Edit** **Delete**

hub — *repo* — Last used on May 05, 2014 — **Edit** **Delete**

guide-issues app — *repo* — Last used on June 16, 2014 — **Edit** **Delete**

⑦ Personal access tokens function like ordinary OAuth access tokens. They can be used instead of a password for Git over HTTPS, or can be used to authenticate to the API over Basic Authentication.

> If you thought all the hardcoded values weren't great, you're right. It is a bad design pattern. We'll remedy this design flaw later in this chapter.

The last bit of Java code that is required is a web controller that serves up a table of issues:

```
package learningspringboot;

import org.springframework.beans.factory.annotation.Autowired;
import org.springframework.stereotype.Controller;
import org.springframework.ui.Model;
import org.springframework.web.bind.annotation.RequestMapping;

@Controller
public class IssueController {

    private IssueManager issueManager;

    @Autowired
    public IssueController(IssueManager issueManager) {
        this.issueManager = issueManager;
    }

    @RequestMapping(value = "/")
    public String index(Model model) {
```

```
        model.addAttribute("issues",
            issueManager.findOpenIssues());
        return "index";
    }
}
```

The class is marked as a Spring MVC `@Controller`. The constructor is tagged `@Autowired`, so when the controller is created by the Spring container, it will initialize its `IssueManager` class using **constructor injection**.

The `index()` method is linked to the web route `"/"` through the `@RequestMapping` annotation. This particular endpoint includes a `Model` parameter, which is automatically supplied by Spring MVC. In this case, it invokes `issueManager.findOpenIssues()` and stores it in the model's `issues` entry. Then, it returns the name of the view to be rendered, which is `index.html`.

Constructor injection is currently the recommended way to wire Spring beans. It supports immutable bean configurations in a better manner and avoids beans getting partially configured at any particular time (http://docs.spring.io/spring/docs/4.0.7.RELEASE/spring-framework-reference/htmlsingle/#beans-dependency-resolution).

The last bit of code we need is a Thymeleaf template created at `src/main/resources/templates/index.html`:

```html
<html xmlns:th="http://www.thymeleaf.org">
<body>
    <p>Open GitHub Issues</p>
    <table>
        <thead>
            <tr>
                <td>Repo</td>
                <td>Issue</td>
                <td>Title</td>
            </tr>
        </thead>
        <tbody>
            <tr th:each="issue : ${issues}">
                <td th:text="${issue.repo}"></td>
                <td>
                    <a th:href="${issue.githubIssue.url}"
                        target="_blank">
                        <span
                            th:text="${issue.githubIssue.number}"/>
                    </a>
                </td>
```

```
            <td th:text="${issue.githubIssue.title}"></td>
          </tr>
        </tbody>
      </table>
    </body>
  </html>
```

There isn't a lot here. The core piece is the dynamically generated table. The template uses a Thymeleaf for-each loop. The `<tr th:each="issue : ${issues}">` tag generates one `<tr>` row for each entry in `${issues}`. From there, we are able to access property values in order to populate text values and URL links, and also show the title of each issue.

We can now run it at this stage! There are a couple of approaches:

- Inside our IDE, we can simply go to `Application` and run `public static void main`. (If you've developed web apps for some time, this is super convenient!)

- The `spring-boot-gradle-plugin` comes with a handy command to run Spring Boot apps.

 Are you using Maven instead of Gradle? Spring Boot has feature parity with `spring-boot-maven-plugin`. Refer to `http://docs.spring.io/spring-boot/docs/1.1.6.RELEASE/reference/htmlsingle/#using-boot-maven-plugin` for more details.

Let's engage `spring-boot-gradle-plugin` by launching the app with Gradle:

```
$ ./gradlew clean bootRun
...

  .   ____          _            __ _ _
 /\\ / ___'_ __ _ _(_)_ __  __ _ \ \ \ \
( ( )\___ | '_ | '_| | '_ \/ _` | \ \ \ \
 \\/  ___)| |_)| | | | | || (_| |  ) ) ) )
  '  |____| .__|_| |_|_| |_\__, | / / / /
 =========|_|==============|___/=/_/_/_/
 :: Spring Boot ::        (v1.1.6.RELEASE)

2014-06-24 23:37:17.164 ... : Starting Application on retina with PID
10443 (/...
2014-06-24 23:37:17.213 ... : Refreshing org.springframework.boot.
context.embe...
2014-06-24 23:37:17.833 ... : Overriding bean definition for bean
```

```
'beanNameVie...
2014-06-24 23:37:18.332 ... : JSR-330 'javax.inject.Inject' annotation
found a...
2014-06-24 23:37:18.750 ... : Server initialized with port: 8080
2014-06-24 23:37:18.993 ... : Starting service Tomcat
2014-06-24 23:37:18.993 ... : Starting Servlet Engine: Apache
Tomcat/7.0.54
2014-06-24 23:37:19.089 ... : Initializing Spring embedded
WebApplicationContext
2014-06-24 23:37:19.089 ... : Root WebApplicationContext: initialization
compl...
2014-06-24 23:37:19.578 ... : Mapping servlet: 'dispatcherServlet' to [/]
2014-06-24 23:37:19.581 ... : Mapping filter: 'hiddenHttpMethodFilter'
to: [/*]
2014-06-24 23:37:19.975 ... : Mapped URL path [/**/favicon.ico] onto
handler o...
2014-06-24 23:37:20.053 ... : Mapped "{[/],methods=[],params=[],headers=[
],con...
2014-06-24 23:37:20.056 ... : Mapped "{[/error],methods=[],params=[],head
ers=[...
2014-06-24 23:37:20.056 ... : Mapped "{[/error],methods=[],params=[],head
ers=[...
2014-06-24 23:37:20.082 ... : Mapped URL path [/**] onto handler of type
[clas...
2014-06-24 23:37:20.083 ... : Mapped URL path [/webjars/**] onto handler
of ty...
2014-06-24 23:37:20.464 ... : Registering beans for JMX exposure on
startup
2014-06-24 23:37:20.502 ... : Tomcat started on port(s): 8080/http
2014-06-24 23:37:20.504 ... : Started Application in 3.896 seconds (JVM
runnin...
```

What is **gradlew**? It's the **gradle wrapper**, which is a handy tool
for any Gradle-based project. Let's assume that you have already
downloaded Gradle from http://www.gradle.org or installed
it using http://gvmtool.net. Inside your project, you can run
gradle wrapper, and it will create a runnable environment with
gradlew and gradlew.bat scripts. Push them out with your project,
and your community won't be obligated to install Gradle. It also lets
you control which version of Gradle is used for your project.

With the app running, we can visit `http://localhost:8080` and see the results.

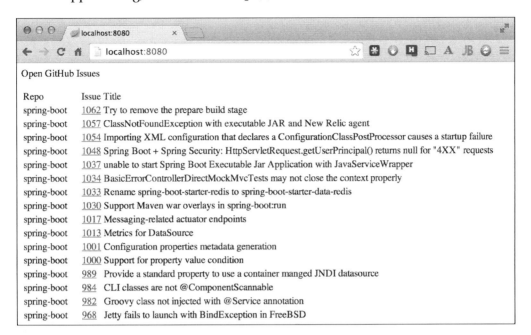

Delving into Spring Boot's property support

In the previous section, we pointed out how hardcoding key attributes is a bad design pattern. Why? It makes it difficult to create updates. It also forces us to build different artifacts for every place our app might be deployed. Certain values such as `githubToken` that should remain secret become visible if our source code is released. Properties and environment variables provide a better alternative location to keep such sensitive and dynamic information.

Java properties and their associated files have existed for a long time, but Java's built-in APIs have always been clunky and require the developer to exert a lot of effort. This probably explains the relative lack of adoption by the industry. Spring Boot revitalizes the core idea behind properties, as we'll see.

The following code is an update to `IssueManager`:

```
package learningspringboot;

import java.util.ArrayList;
import java.util.List;
```

```java
import org.springframework.beans.factory.InitializingBean;
import org.springframework.beans.factory.annotation.Value;
import org.springframework.social.github.api.GitHubIssue;
import org.springframework.social.github.api.impl.GitHubTemplate;
import org.springframework.stereotype.Service;

@Service
public class IssueManager implements InitializingBean {

    @Value("${github.token}")
    String githubToken;

    @Value("${org}")
    String org;

    @Value("${repos}")
    String[] repos;

    GitHubTemplate gitHubTemplate;

    @Override
    public void afterPropertiesSet() throws Exception {
        this.gitHubTemplate = new GitHubTemplate(githubToken);
    }

    public List<Issue> findOpenIssues() {
        List<Issue> openIssues = new ArrayList<>();

        for (String repo : repos) {
            for (GitHubIssue issue : gitHubTemplate
                    .repoOperations().getIssues(org, repo)) {
                if (issue.getState().equals("open")) {
                    openIssues.add(new Issue(repo, issue));
                }
            }
        }

        return openIssues;

    }
}
```

This version is almost the same as the previous `IssueManager` class. The difference is that we are using Spring's `@Value` annotation to glean properties instead of hardcoding them. Any of these newly defined properties can be injected from multiple sources. They are cascaded in the following order:

- Default values can be supplied directly with `@Value("${propertyName:def` `aultValue}")`
- `@Value` defaults can be overridden in an `application.properties` file, which gets bundled with the app in a JAR file
- Bundled properties can be overridden in an auxiliary `application.` `properties` file adjacent to the deployed JAR
- Auxiliary properties can be overridden by environment variables, either from the command line, a `.bashrc` file, or Windows environment settings
- In a cloud environment, environment variables can be supplied by the configuration, as we'll see toward the end of this chapter

Our code also creates `GitHubTemplate` using Spring's `InitializingBean` interface. The `afterPropertiesSet` method is called after all properties are configured by Spring's IoC container. This ensures that `githubToken` is populated when we create the template.

As we don't have default values, we need to create `src/main/resources/` `application.properties`:

```
org=spring-projects
repos=spring-boot,spring-boot-issues
```

Let's see what is happening:

- `org`: This is set to `spring-projects`. Our app's `GitHubTemplate` instance will use this to query `https://github.com/spring-projects`.
- `repos`: This is converted by Spring into `String[]{"spring-boot",` `"spring-boot-issues"}`.

As a bonus, Spring Boot provides relaxed rules on name binding. This means that we can set `githubToken` using either `github.token` or `GITHUB_TOKEN` as command-line environment variables. This provides universal support on *nix, Mac, and Windows. There is no need to write any code to process properties files!

Let's try out the latter approach:

```
$ GITHUB_TOKEN=ccdbf257f052a594a0e7bd2823a69ae38a48ffb1 ./gradlew clean
bootRun
```

In firing up this app, we provided a command-line value for GITHUB_TOKEN. Our app is preloaded with an opinion on the settings. However, we have the flexibility to quickly override these values in production—should the need arise—and critical security details are kept out of our source code.

 It's still the developer's responsibility to *not* add github.token to src/main/resources/application.properties and then push it to a publicly visible repository.

Adding server-side mobile support with Spring Mobile

So, we have a nicely functioning app that fetches GitHub issues. What can we do to take this example to the next level and explore Spring Boot? Considering that many companies are seeing their primary Internet traffic come from mobile consumers, what if we added mobile support to our app?

Spring Boot comes with out-of-the-box support for this. Just add the following dependency to build.gradle:

```
compile("org.springframework.boot:spring-boot-starter-mobile")
```

This pulls in **Spring Mobile** (http://projects.spring.io/spring-mobile), which is a library that easily switches between different views based on the browsing client's user agent.

First, add this line to src/main/resources/application.properties:

```
spring.mobile.devicedelegatingviewresolver.enabled=true
```

By default, mobile support is switched off. This value activates Spring Mobile's ability to switch views based on a user agent lookup.

Other settings are available, as listed in the following snippet:

```
spring.mobile.devicedelegatingviewresolver.normalPrefix=
spring.mobile.devicedelegatingviewresolver.normalSuffix=
```

```
spring.mobile.devicedelegatingviewresolver.mobilePrefix=mobile/
spring.mobile.devicedelegatingviewresolver.mobileSuffix=
spring.mobile.devicedelegatingviewresolver.tabletPrefix=tablet/
spring.mobile.devicedelegatingviewresolver.tabletSuffix=
```

 These are the defaults inside Spring Boot and are not in our app.

These settings can be overridden either in our own `application.properties` file or later on, as described previously.

 While the tablet prefix is configured, we are going to focus solely on mobiles in this chapter.

This is good. The default template, which is `src/main/resources/templates/index.html`, is the same as before. However, with the new `mobile/` prefix, we need to create `src/main/resources/templates/mobile/index.html`:

```html
<html xmlns:th="http://www.thymeleaf.org">
<body>
    <p>Open GitHub Issues - Mobile</p>
</body>
</html>
```

There's not much here. For the moment, it just displays an alternate message, which indicates that we hit the right view. We'll add to it later in this chapter. Let's just see how it switches views properly; it's time to fire it up.

Are we ready to test things out? Well, not quite yet. Spring Mobile uses the browser's user agent to make decisions based on the type of screen that is viewing the site. While we can use a real mobile device to test things out, this process can be quite cumbersome and time consuming. It's best to find a plugin for our browser in order to switch the user agent settings automatically.

Ultimate Agent Sniffer (http://iblogbox.com/chrome/useragent/alert.php) is one tool that lets you easily switch a browser tab to an iPad, iPhone, or just about any other device you can think of. However, it's not the only one. You can find one that suits your needs. The following screenshot shows you how to configure the current browser tab on an iPhone 4:

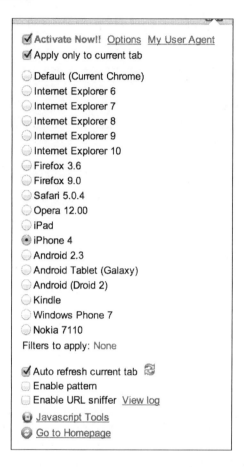

With the app running and our browser switched to mobile view, let's visit http://localhost:8080.

We can see the `mobile/index.html` template with ease. Things are lined up in order to create a truly mobile experience!

Creating a mobile frontend with jQuery Mobile

Mobile apps seem to be taking over the world. If a website doesn't provide a friendly mobile view, then people don't seem to like it. As we build web apps all the time, it's critical to create a frontend UI that is usable. jQuery Mobile is a handy toolkit that gets UIs up and running quickly.

 This is merely a quick introduction to jQuery Mobile. For something more comprehensive, please read *jQuery Mobile Web Development Essentials* by *Raymond Camden* and *Andy Matthews*.

In the previous chapter, we took a quick glance at **Bower** (`http://bower.io`), which is a package manager for JavaScript libraries. We will use it to install jQuery Mobile into our app. Assuming that we have already installed Bower, let's proceed to define where Bower will put the packages by creating a `.bowerrc` file in the root of our project. This file will signal Bower to put all of our JavaScript modules into `src/main/resources/public/`, where Spring Boot can automatically serve them up:

```
{
    "directory": "src/main/resources/public/"
}
```

In the previous chapter, we dropped the files into `public/`. In this case, as we have a conventional Gradle project layout, the same target folder is at `src/main/resources/`. By the way, we have the same options (`/META-INF/resources/`, `/resources/`, `/static/`, `/public/`). We simply have to place them at `src/main/resources/`.

Looks like we're ready to go! Execute the following steps:

```
$ bower init
[?] name: issue-manager
[?] version: 0.1.0
[?] description: Learning Spring Boot - Issue Manager
[?] main file:
[?] what types of modules does this package expose? amd
```

```
[?] keywords:

[?] authors: Greg Turnquist <gturnquist@pivotal.io>

[?] license: ASL

[?] homepage: http://blog.greglturnquist.com/category/learning-spring-
boot

[?] set currently installed components as dependencies? No

[?] add commonly ignored files to ignore list? Yes

[?] would you like to mark this package as private, which prevents it
from being accidentally published to the registry? Yes

...

[?] Looks good? Yes
```

With this setup, let's now install jQuery Mobile:

```
$ bower install jquery-mobile-bower --save

bower jquery-mobile-bower#*      cached git://github.com/jobrapido/jquery-
mobile-bower.git#1.4.2

bower jquery-mobile-bower#*    validate 1.4.2 against git://github.com/
jobrapido/jquery-mobile-bower.git#*

bower jquery#~1.10.0              cached git://github.com/jquery/jquery.
git#1.10.2

bower jquery#~1.10.0              validate 1.10.2 against git://github.com/
jquery/jquery.git#~1.10.0

bower jquery-mobile-bower#~1.4.2              install jquery-mobile-
bower#1.4.2

bower jquery#~1.10.0                          install jquery#1.10.2


jquery-mobile-bower#1.4.2 src/main/resources/public/jquery-mobile-bower
└── jquery#1.10.2


jquery#1.10.2 src/main/resources/public/jquery
```

We can see that it installed jQuery Mobile 1.4.2 along with jQuery 1.10.0. This gives us all we need in order to craft a mobile web page.

 Again, this isn't a complete introduction to jQuery Mobile. A great resource for learning how to drive various widgets is jQuery Mobile's showcase, which is available at http://demos.jquerymobile.com/1.4.2.

To see our complete lineup of JavaScript modules for the frontend, check out
`bower.json`:

```
{
  "name": "issue-manager",
  "version": "0.1.0",
  "authors": [
    "Greg Turnquist <gturnquist@pivotal.io>"
  ],
  "description": "Learning Spring Boot - Issue Manager",
  "license": "ASL",
  "homepage": "http://blog.greglturnquist.com/category/learning-
    spring-boot",
  "private": true,
  "ignore": [
    "**/.*",
    "node_modules",
    "bower_components",
    "src/main/resources/public/",
    "test",
    "tests"
  ],
  "dependencies": {
    "jquery-mobile-bower": "~1.4.2"
  }
}
```

It's time to put the pedal to the metal and load up jQuery Mobile's CSS and
JavaScript components. The following page is a very simple mobile layout that
we need to create at `src/main/resources/templates/mobile/index.html`:

```
<html xmlns:th="http://www.thymeleaf.org">
<head>
    <meta name="viewport" content="width=device-width, initial-
        scale=1" />
    <link rel="stylesheet" href="jquery-mobile-
        bower/css/jquery.mobile-1.4.2.css" />
    <script src="jquery/jquery.js"></script>
    <script src="jquery-mobile-bower/js/jquery.mobile-
        1.4.2.js"></script>
</head>
<body>
    <div data-role="page" id="home">

        <div data-role="header" data-position="fixed">
```

```
            <a href="/" data-icon="home" data-
                iconpos="notext"></a>
            <h1>Issue Manager Mobile</h1>
        </div>

        <div data-role="content">
            <ul data-role="listview">
                <li th:each="issue : ${issues}">
                    <a th:href="${issue.githubIssue.htmlUrl}"
                        target="_blank"
                      th:text="${issue.githubIssue.title}">
                    </a>
                </li>
            </ul>
        </div>

    </div>
</body>
</html>
```

Where do we begin? Okay, maybe it's a little bit bigger than you expected. However, if you've done any major hacking on HTML, you might recognize that this isn't as huge as other frontend systems. So, let's break it up:

```
<html xmlns:th="http://www.thymeleaf.org">
```

The first line is a giveaway that this is most certainly a Thymeleaf template. It declares the th namespace, and we plan to take full advantage of this later in the code:

```
<head>
    <meta name="viewport" content="width=device-width, initial-
        scale=1" />
    <link rel="stylesheet" href="jquery-mobile-
        bower/css/jquery.mobile-1.4.2.css" />
    <script src="jquery/jquery.js"></script>
    <script src="jquery-mobile-bower/js/jquery.mobile-
        1.4.2.js"></script>
</head>
```

The header section starts off by creating some viewport settings. Essentially, it's saying that the browser should use the full width of the device and that we are completely zoomed in. Double-tapping the screen of your phone won't cause it to zoom in any more. Next, we are loading up jQuery Mobile's CSS style sheet. Then, we load up jQuery and jQuery Mobile JavaScript modules.

Now, let's look at the `<body>` part of the page:

```
<body>
    <div data-role="page" id="home">

        <div data-role="header" data-position="fixed">
            <a href="/" data-icon="home" data-
                iconpos="notext"></a>
            <h1>Issue Manager Mobile</h1>
        </div>

        <div data-role="content">
            <ul data-role="listview">
                <li th:each="issue : ${issues}">
                    <a th:href="${issue.githubIssue.htmlUrl}"
                        target="_blank"
                      th:text="${issue.githubIssue.title}">
                    </a>
                </li>
            </ul>
        </div>

    </div>
</body>
</html>
```

jQuery Mobile is a declarative toolkit, which means that we only have to lay out a set of key elements, and when the package finishes loading it will apply mobile CSS styling. In this case, we have a top level `<div data-role="page" id="home">` tag, which defines a mobile "page." The term "page" is wrapped in scary quotes because it isn't the same thing as an HTML page. jQuery Mobile can support multiple pages and will only display the current one.

 As this is a single page app, we aren't going any deeper into multiple pages. Instead, we'll focus on the other parts.

Inside the "home" page, there is a `<div data-role="header" data-position="fixed">` tag. This fragment defines what appears at the top. Basically, a header can show up to three components on the device: the left, the middle, and the right. In our case, there is an anchor tag and a header. This automatically gets shifted to the left and middle spots upon rendering. The anchor tag will be rendered as a button but with a home icon instead of any text. The `header` tag takes the middle slot. For our example, there isn't anything that can be put in the right slot.

After this, we get to the meat of the page: `<div data-role="content">`. This is the content and is where most of the device's real estate will be put to work. It's very analogous to the desktop version of things. The exception is that instead of a table with rows, we are creating a list view of listed items. jQuery Mobile will convert every line item into a button.

The anchor tag inside the list item has the URL. When you click on one of these mobile buttons, it will open a new tab in our browser. The button's text shows you the title as the text value.

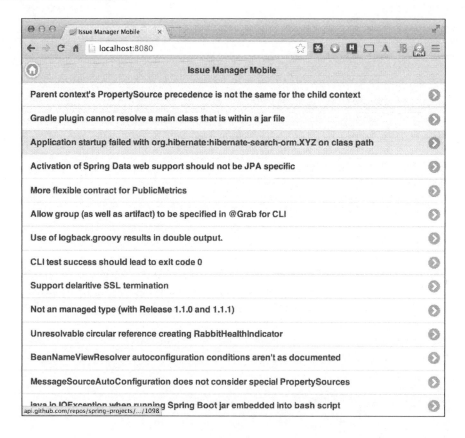

This seems to do the trick! Using our desktop browser and Ultimate User Agent Switcher has made it easy to build this mobile frontend. However, nothing is complete without a check from a *real* mobile device. We'll see how to do this a bit later.

Bundling up the application as a runnable JAR

In the previous chapter, we learned how to run Groovy scripts with Spring Boot's CLI tool. This empowered us to create runnable JAR files, which can be deployed anywhere a JVM is installed. In this chapter, let's see how a Java-based project can be bundled up as a JAR and deployed to a popular PaaS provider.

Spring Boot comes with two handy plugins: `spring-boot-maven-plugin` and `spring-boot-gradle-plugin`. As we are using Gradle in this book, the project file from `start.spring.io` has `spring-boot-gradle-plugin` installed. Earlier, we ran the app from the command line using `./gradlew bootRun`. To bundle up a JAR file, we merely need to do this:

```
$ ./gradlew clean build
:clean
:compileJava
:processResources
:classes
:jar
:bootRepackage
:assemble
:compileTestJava UP-TO-DATE
:processTestResources UP-TO-DATE
:testClasses UP-TO-DATE
:test UP-TO-DATE
:check UP-TO-DATE
:build

BUILD SUCCESSFUL

Total time: 7.168 secs
```

Did you get an error from Gradle? `start.spring.io` creates `ApplicationTests`, which will fail due to the required `github.token` property. As we aren't focused on writing automated tests, the simplest thing to do is to delete this `test` class and try again. Pay heed to the fact that skipping unit tests is *not* recommended for a real production app.

Spring Boot initially builds a traditional JAR file. This file contains the compiled class files, all the public resource files such as our jQuery Mobile code and HTML templates, and the `pom` file. We can find it at `build/libs/issue-manager-0.0.1-SNAPSHOT.jar.original`. This JAR file isn't runnable. In fact, it doesn't even have third-party dependencies; this is by design. Such a JAR file can only be used to build a bigger artifact, such as a WAR file.

In the spirit of runnable apps, Spring Boot's plugin takes another step. It creates a new JAR file based on the original one and then adds third-party dependencies and some support code in order to load the libraries. This can be found at `build/libs/issue-manager-0.0.1-SNAPSHOT.jar`:

```
$ ls build/libs
issue-manager-0.0.1-SNAPSHOT.jar
issue-manager-0.0.1-SNAPSHOT.jar.original
```

We can fire up the JAR file now:

```
$ GITHUB_TOKEN=ccdbf257f052a594a0e7bd2823a69ae38a48ffb1 java -jar build/
libs/i...

  .   ____          _            __ _ _
 /\\ / ___'_ __ _ _(_)_ __  __ _ \ \ \ \
( ( )\___ | '_ | '_| | '_ \/ _` | \ \ \ \
 \\/  ___)| |_)| | | | | || (_| |  ) ) ) )
  '  |____| .__|_| |_|_| |_\__, | / / / /
 =========|_|==============|___/=/_/_/_/
 :: Spring Boot ::        (v1.1.6.RELEASE)

2014-06-24 23:48:38.119 ... : Starting Application on retina with PID
10542 (/...
2014-06-24 23:48:38.182 ... : Refreshing org.springframework.boot.
context.embe...
2014-06-24 23:48:38.775 ... : Overriding bean definition for bean
'beanNameVie...
```

```
2014-06-24 23:48:39.278 ... : JSR-330 'javax.inject.Inject' annotation
found a...
2014-06-24 23:48:39.864 ... : Server initialized with port: 8080
2014-06-24 23:48:40.156 ... : Starting service Tomcat
2014-06-24 23:48:40.157 ... : Starting Servlet Engine: Apache
Tomcat/7.0.54
2014-06-24 23:48:40.288 ... : Initializing Spring embedded
WebApplicationContext
2014-06-24 23:48:40.289 ... : Root WebApplicationContext: initialization
compl...
2014-06-24 23:48:40.935 ... : Mapping servlet: 'dispatcherServlet' to [/]
2014-06-24 23:48:40.938 ... : Mapping filter: 'hiddenHttpMethodFilter'
to: [/*]
2014-06-24 23:48:41.687 ... : Mapped URL path [/**/favicon.ico] onto
handler o...
2014-06-24 23:48:41.803 ... : Mapped "{[/],methods=[],params=[],headers=[
],con...
2014-06-24 23:48:41.805 ... : Mapped "{[/error],methods=[],params=[],head
ers=[...
2014-06-24 23:48:41.805 ... : Mapped "{[/error],methods=[],params=[],head
ers=[...
2014-06-24 23:48:41.831 ... : Mapped URL path [/**] onto handler of type
[clas...
2014-06-24 23:48:41.831 ... : Mapped URL path [/webjars/**] onto handler
of ty...
2014-06-24 23:48:42.042 ... : Registering beans for JMX exposure on
startup
2014-06-24 23:48:42.106 ... : Tomcat started on port(s): 8080/http
2014-06-24 23:48:42.107 ... : Started Application in 4.513 seconds (JVM
runnin...
```

Now we can visit `http://localhost:8080` and either view the desktop version or the mobile version. If we check for the local IP address of our machine, we can view it from a mobile device that's on the same Wi-Fi network.

 If you are on a Mac or *nix system, it's possible to find the local IP address by typing `ifconfig | grep inet | grep -v 127.0.0.1`.

Assuming that we get our computer and phone on the same network, we can easily view the mobile version of the app.

We can see the list of tickets open on the GitHub repositories. If we click on one, it will take us to GitHub, where we can easily view the details of the issue.

Deploying to Cloud Foundry

One popular PaaS (Platform as a Service) provider is Cloud Foundry. You can visit a public-facing version known as Pivotal Web Services at `https://run.pivotal.io` to discover options. It's also possible for you to build and set up your own local instance of Cloud Foundry using the open source tools found at `https://github.com/cloudfoundry`, but we won't go into that. Assuming that you have an account at `run.pivotal.io`, let's proceed by installing the Cloud Foundry CLI tool.

If we visit `https://github.com/cloudfoundry/cli`, we can find installation instructions for multiple platforms.

On a Mac system with Homebrew (`http://brew.sh`), all we have to do is type the following:

```
$ brew tap pivotal/tap
$ brew install cloudfoundry-cli
```

```
==> Downloading https://downloads.sf.net/project/machomebrew/Bottles/
cloudfoundry-cli-6.1.1.mavericks.bottle.tar.gz
```

```
Already downloaded: /Library/Caches/Homebrew/cloudfoundry-cli-
6.1.1.mavericks.bottle.tar.gz
```

```
==> Pouring cloudfoundry-cli-6.1.1.mavericks.bottle.tar.gz
```

From here, we can log in to CF:

```
$ cf login
API endpoint: https://api.run.pivotal.io


Email> gturnquist@pivotal.io


Password>
Authenticating...
OK


API endpoint: https://api.run.pivotal.io (API version: 2.6.0)
User:        gturnquist@pivotal.io
Org:         FrameworksAndRuntimes
Space:       development
```

We are prompted for the API endpoint. In Pivotal's commercial instance of CF, this will be `https://api.run.pivotal.io`. If you are running a different instance, your API endpoint will be different. We must then use our e-mail/password credentials. After getting in, we might have to pick our organization and space for deployment. In all likelihood, your options will be different than what's shown in the preceding console output.

At this point, we can deploy our app as follows:

```
$ cf push issue-manager-gturnquist -p target/issue-manager-0.0.1-
SNAPSHOT.jar -m 512M
Creating app issue-manager-gturnquist in org FrameworksAndRuntimes /
space development as gturnquist@pivotal.io...
OK


Creating route issue-manager-gturnquist.cfapps.io...
OK


Binding issue-manager-gturnquist.cfapps.io to issue-manager-gturnquist...
```

```
OK


Uploading issue-manager-gturnquist...

Uploading app files from: target/issue-manager-0.0.1-SNAPSHOT.jar

Uploading 1.7M, 474 files

OK


Starting app issue-manager-gturnquist in org FrameworksAndRuntimes /
space development as gturnquist@pivotal.io...

OK

-----> Downloaded app package (13M)

-----> Java Buildpack Version: v2.1.2 | https://github.com/cloudfoundry/
java-buildpack.git#074fd9a

-----> Downloading Open Jdk JRE 1.8.0_60 from http://download.run.
pivotal.io/openjdk/lucid/x86_64/openjdk-1.8.0_60.tar.gz (1.4s)

       Expanding Open Jdk JRE to .java-buildpack/open_jdk_jre (1.0s)

-----> Downloading Spring Auto Reconfiguration 0.8.9 from http://
download.run.pivotal.io/auto-reconfiguration/auto-reconfiguration-
0.8.9.jar (0.0s)

-----> Uploading droplet (44M)


0 of 1 instances running, 1 starting

...

0 of 1 instances running, 1 down

0 of 1 instances running, 1 failing

FAILED

Start unsuccessful


NOTE: use 'cf logs issue-manager-gturnquist --recent' for more
information
```

First, let's examine the arguments used to push our app to CF:

- The app name is `issue-manager-gturnquist`.

- The artifact was supplied with `-p target/issue-manager-0.0.1-SNAPSHOT.jar`.

- The memory was increased to 512 MB. It has been observed that Spring Boot apps need more than the minimum memory for web-based apps. (Why? I'm not sure at the time of writing this.)

However, wait a second; `cf` says that the deployment failed! Why is that? Well, it appears to be giving us a clue by showing us how to check the logfiles:

```
$ cf logs issue-manager-gturnquist --recent

...

2014-06-15T00:35:23.45-0500 [App/0]   ... Could not resolve placeholder
'github.token' in string value "${github.token}"

...
```

Ah ha! We don't have the `github.token` property configured. In all the other examples of running this app, whether using `./gradlew bootRun` or by running the executable JAR file, we supplied that value. So what do we do in this situation? Simple:

```
$ cf set-env issue-manager-gturnquist GITHUB_TOKEN
ccdbf257f052a594a0e7bd2823a69ae38a48ffb1

Setting env variable 'GITHUB_TOKEN' to
'ccdbf257f052a594a0e7bd2823a69ae38a48ffb1' for app issue-manager-
gturnquist...
OK
NOTE: Use 'cf push' to ensure your env variable changes take effect
```

Okay, we've supplied an environmental variable that will be associated with the cloud-hosted instance of this app. We can push updated JAR files all we want. As long as we don't delete the remote app flat out, it's environmental settings will stick:

```
$ cf push issue-manager-gturnquist -p target/issue-manager-0.0.1-
SNAPSHOT.jar

...

0 of 1 instances running, 1 starting
0 of 1 instances running, 1 starting
0 of 1 instances running, 1 starting
1 of 1 instances running


App started


Showing health and status for app issue-manager-gturnquist in org
FrameworksAndRuntimes / space development as gturnquist@pivotal.io...
OK


requested state: started
instances: 1/1
```

```
usage: 512M x 1 instances
urls: issue-manager-gturnquist.cfapps.io
```

	state	since	cpu	memory	disk
#0	running	2014-06-15 12:38:26 AM	0.0%	251.4M of 512M	108.3M of
1G					

 We didn't supply the memory argument this time, because that information is already stored with the app, just like GITHUB_TOKEN.

Now, we can visit http://issue-manager-gturnquist.cfapps.io.

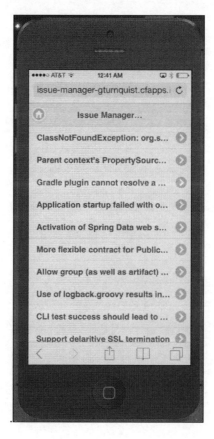

Perfect! This looks identical to what we saw earlier, except that we don't have to visit port 8080, and it's available anywhere on the Internet.

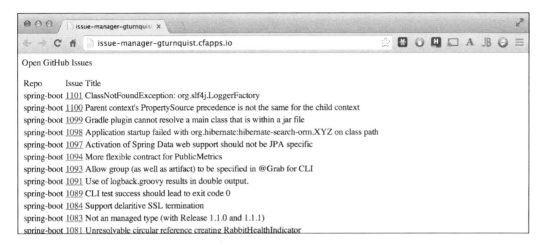

If we visit the same site from our desktop browser, we can see the original look and feel.

Adding production-ready support

So, is anything missing? Well, in the previous chapter, we added @Grab("spring-boot-actuator") and @Grab("spring-boot-starter-remote-shell"), and it created a slew of extra HTTP endpoints. While Gradle isn't quite as concise as Groovy Grape, it's not that hard. Just add the following dependencies to build.gradle:

```
compile("org.springframework.boot:spring-boot-starter-actuator")
compile("org.springframework.boot:spring-boot-starter-remote-shell")
```

These two Spring Boot starters activate Spring Boot Actuator as well the CRaSH remote shell support.

In the previous chapter, we saw some detailed screenshots and explored how to view these endpoints in our browser. All this is quite useful. However, one thing that was mentioned was the possibility of writing a script in order to consume the metrics. What would it take to start gathering metric data every second and dump it into a CSV file that can be read with Excel? Let's start by creating an independent script called `metrics.groovy` in the root folder of our project:

```groovy
package learningspringboot

@Grab("groovy-all")
import groovy.json.*

@EnableScheduling
class MetricsCollector {

    def url = "http://localhost:8080/metrics"
    def slurper = new JsonSlurper()
    def keys = slurper.parse(new URL(url)).keySet()
        .findAll{
            it.startsWith("counter")
        }
    def header = false;

    @Scheduled(fixedRate = 1000L)
    void run() {
        if (!header) {
            println(keys.join(','))
            header = true
        }

        def metrics = slurper.parse(new URL(url))

        println(keys.collect{metrics[it]}.join(','))
    }

}
```

So, what is buried in this gem of a script? Take a look:

- `@Grab("groovy-all")` brings the vast wealth of Groovy on board (most notably, JsonSlurper)
- We initialize a connection to `http://localhost:8080/metrics` and then fetch all keys that start with `counter`

- @EnableScheduling turns on Spring's ability to have scheduled method calls; run() is booked to run every 1000 ms
- The first time run() executes, it will print out a header with each key's name joined by commas (the CSV format)
- Every other time run() is executed, it reconnects to http:// localhost:8080/metrics in order to download and parse the data
- Finally, using the list of keys, each data point is gathered and printed out, spliced together by commas (CSV)

To use the script, we first need to fire up our new and improved Issue Manager app with Spring Boot Actuator turned on:

```
$ GITHUB_TOKEN=ccdbf257f052a594a0e7bd2823a69ae38a48ffb1 ./gradlew clean
bootRun
```

With the Actuator up and running, we can now launch our metrics collection script in another shell (in the same folder in which metrics.groovy lives):

```
$ spring run -q metrics.groovy | tee metrics.csv
counter.status.200.autoconfig,counter.status.200.beans,counter.
status.200.conf...
1,1,1,1,1,1,1,1,21,1,2,1
1,1,1,1,1,1,1,1,22,1,2,1
1,1,1,1,1,1,1,1,23,1,2,1
1,1,1,1,1,1,1,1,24,1,2,1
1,1,1,1,1,1,1,1,25,1,2,1
1,1,1,1,1,1,1,1,26,1,2,1
1,1,1,1,1,1,1,1,27,1,2,1
1,1,1,1,1,1,1,1,28,1,2,1
1,1,1,1,1,1,1,1,29,1,2,1
1,1,1,1,1,1,1,1,30,1,2,1
1,1,1,1,1,1,1,1,31,1,2,1
1,1,1,1,1,1,1,1,32,1,2,1
1,1,1,1,1,1,1,1,33,1,2,1
1,1,1,1,1,1,1,1,34,1,2,1
1,1,1,1,1,1,1,1,35,1,2,1
1,1,1,1,1,1,1,1,36,1,2,1
```

Assuming we have done that, we can now open `metrics.csv` using Excel.

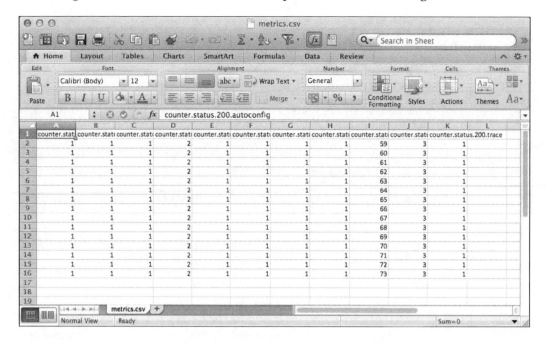

Gee, that's no fun. The only metrics that are increasing appear to be our script hitting /metrics. Well, duh! If only there was a way to automatically visit other sites. Oh, but there is! Groovy is a powerful platform. Why don't we write a script that can load test our website at the same time? Let's do this as follows:

```
package learningspringboot

@Grab('org.codehaus.gpars:gpars:1.1.0')
import groovyx.gpars.GParsPool
import groovy.util.logging.*

@Slf4j
class LoadTester implements CommandLineRunner {

    void run(String[] args) {
        GParsPool.withPool(8) {
            def loadset = ["http://localhost:8080"]*100
            loadset.eachParallel { url ->
                def results = url.toURL().text
                log.info("Hit ${url}")
            }
        }
    }

}
```

So, what's all this? It's not that long, but it's packed with lots of features:

- `GPars` (`http://gpars.codehaus.org/`) is the Groovy Parallel Systems library. We're using it to perform parallel load testing
- This script implements Spring Boot's `CommandLineRunner` interface, so it will invoke the `run()` method
- `GParsPool.withPool(8)` creates a parallel pool with eight workers (because I happen to have an eight-core laptop)
- Inside this block, we create an array with 100 instances of `http://localhost:8080`, which is the root URL of issue manager
- With this array of addresses, we ask GPars to iterate over every entry using `eachParallel { }` in parallel
- Inside each iteration, we convert `url` into `java.net.URL`, connect, and fetch the text of the page
- Instead of printing out the content, we are effectively just clicking on the URL

This effectively hits the website 100 times, as fast as eight cores can go. Looking at the following metrics screenshot, we can see that `counter.status.200.root` is now up to **100**.

With this setup, let's launch `spring run metrics.groovy | tee metrics.csv` in one shell while we run `spring run load_test.groovy` in another.

This screenshot nicely shows our metrics counter results, gathered in a persistent spreadsheet:

	A1	fx	counter.status.200.metrics

	A	B	C	D
1	counter.status.200.metrics	counter.status.200.root		
2	23	22		
3	24	23		
4	25	24		
5	26	25		
6	27	26		
7	28	26		
8	29	26		
9	30	26		
10	31	28		
11	32	29		
12	33	29		
13	34	31		
14	35	32		
15	36	32		
16	37	33		
17	38	33		
18	39	34		

Here, we can see that `metrics.csv` has counts of both `counters.status.200.metrics` and `counters.status.200.root`.

For production-ready support, it's nice that Actuator provides us handy data that we can consume. The scripts that we used in order to consume these metrics might seem a bit crude. However, in the real world, we need tools that let us quickly try something out before investing in bigger, more complex, and often more expensive solutions.

If our manager wanted a quick read of the last 24 hours of data, we could easily take `metrics.groovy` and adjust it to have a rolling time limit. We could then serve up the content using a little Spring MVC. Cash in on Spring MVC's WebSocket support, and we could have the screens update dynamically. Program managers love eye candy, right?

There's no telling what requirements we'll get from system administrators and managers. Spring Boot's easy-to-consume endpoints provide us with the tools we need in our main application as well as the support tools we'll build in order to manage things.

Summary

In this chapter, we used `http://start.spring.io` to create a bare bones project with Gradle support. We plugged in Spring Social GitHub and used it to scan multiple repositories for open issues. Then, we used Spring Mobile and jQuery Mobile to create an alternative mobile frontend. We learned how to use Spring Boot's über easy property support. We bundled it up into a runnable JAR file and deployed it to Cloud Foundry. Finally, we added production-ready support and did a little bit of load testing while gathering metrics.

In the next chapter, we will explore all the tools at our disposal that can be used to debug and manage Spring Boot applications.

3
Debugging and Managing Your App

"I have two hours today to build an app from scratch. @springboot to the rescue!"

— *John Ferguson* `@fergusonjohnw`

So you've decided to build an application using Spring Boot? Sooner or later, something will go wrong. It does not matter how experienced we are. How will Spring Boot help us figure out what went wrong and fix things? This chapter introduces lots of tools to help us debug and manage "bootiful" apps (a term coined by Josh Long).

In this chapter, we will learn the following topics:

- Creating a JMS-based publisher/subscriber app using embedded ActiveMQ
- Viewing the auto-configuration report and figuring out what was/wasn't configured automatically
- Overriding some of Boot's settings by properties and putting them in alternate bean definitions in the code
- Providing custom health checks (such as pinging ActiveMQ's broker)
- Customizing the data shown at `/info` by plugging in things such as app name and version
- Creating custom metrics to track the number of messages published and consumed
- Changing the port, address, and path of management endpoints
- Disabling HTTP-based management endpoints falling back to JMX
- Connecting to JMX via JConsole and jmxterm
- Adding the CRaSH remote shell and creating custom commands

Creating a JMS-based publisher/subscriber app

To dig in and see how to debug an application, let's put together something simple: an app that monitors incoming messages from the network. These messages can indicate different levels of network degradation or recovery as reported by various devices.

For a pretty basic JMS-based app that runs on top of ActiveMQ, we can use the following `build.gradle` build file:

```
buildscript {
    repositories {
        mavenCentral()
    }
    dependencies {
        classpath("org.springframework.boot:spring-boot-gradle-
        plugin:1.1.6.RELEASE")
    }
}

apply plugin: 'java'
apply plugin: 'spring-boot'

jar {
    baseName = 'network-monitor'
    version =  '0.0.1-SNAPSHOT'
}

sourceCompatibility = 1.8
targetCompatibility = 1.8

repositories {
    mavenCentral()
}

// tag::clean[]
clean {
    delete "activemq-data"
}
// end::clean[]
```

```
dependencies {
    compile("org.springframework.boot:spring-boot-starter")
    compile("org.springframework:spring-jms")
    compile("org.apache.activemq:activemq-broker")
}

task wrapper(type: Wrapper) {
    gradleVersion = '2.1'
}
```

 This app uses Java 8, even though Spring Boot supports versions all the way back to Java 6.

This app uses basic `spring-boot-starter`. It also pulls in `spring-jms` and `activemq-broker`. In the past, we would have plugged in Joda-Time; however, with Java 8, we have a new and improved API. With all this in place, it's time to slug out some code:

```
package learningspringboot;

import java.io.Serializable;
import java.time.LocalDateTime;

public class Alarm implements Serializable {

    final private String hostname;
    final private LocalDateTime eventTime;
    final private Severity severity;

    public Alarm(String hostname, LocalDateTime eventTime,
    Severity severity) {
        this.hostname = hostname;
        this.eventTime = eventTime;
        this.severity = severity;
    }

    public String getHostname() {
        return hostname;
    }

    public LocalDateTime getEventTime() {
```

```
            return eventTime;
    }

    public Severity getSeverity() {
        return severity;
    }

    public String toString() {
        return "Event[" + hostname + ":" + severity + "]";
    }
}
```

This domain object is at the heart of our network monitoring app. It represents an alarm occurring somewhere in the network. The domain object contains the hostname of the reporting device, the time the event occurred, and the severity of the alarm. It's designed to be created only through a constructor call. This makes the data immutable and forces the user to create the domain object in a complete and stable state. It also implements the `Serializable` interface so that we can serialize instances of these events and transmit them through a message broker. Also, we have a custom `toString` method to print out its contents.

 While we will probably want the `eventTime` included in `toString` in real life, it's been removed to make output easier to read further down in this chapter.

The `Alarm` class contains a custom `Severity` type as follows:

```
package learningspringboot;

public enum Severity {

    UP, DEGRADED, JEOPARDY, DOWN
}
```

The severity of the alarm could have been something simpler like an integer. However, it's often hard to remember what is good versus bad when you use values such as one and five. Instead, we have defined a Java `enum`. This way, the severity of the alarm is very clear and well defined.

In this chapter, we don't need to access a real network to demo Spring Boot's features. Instead, let's create a simulator as follows:

```
package learningspringboot;

import java.time.LocalDateTime;
```

```java
import java.util.Random;

import org.springframework.jms.core.JmsTemplate;
import org.springframework.scheduling.annotation.Scheduled;

public class NetworkEventSimulator {

    final private JmsTemplate jmsTemplate;
    final private String destination;

    public NetworkEventSimulator(JmsTemplate jmsTemplate, String
    dest) {
        this.jmsTemplate = jmsTemplate;
        this.destination = dest;
    }

    @Scheduled(fixedRate = 1000L)
    public void simulateActivity() {

        Random random = new Random();

        String hostname;
        switch (random.nextInt(3)) {
            case 0: hostname = "router101"; break;
            case 1: hostname = "multiplex205"; break;
            default: hostname = "switch1143"; break;
        }

        Severity severity;
        switch (random.nextInt(4)) {
            case 0: severity = Severity.UP; break;
            case 1: severity = Severity.DEGRADED; break;
            case 2: severity = Severity.JEOPARDY; break;
            default: severity = Severity.DOWN; break;
        }
        Alarm event = new Alarm(hostname, LocalDateTime.now(),
                severity);
        jmsTemplate.convertAndSend(destination, event);
    }

}
```

The simulator expects to be supplied with both `jmsTemplate` and `destination` instances.

In this case, we are using Spring's scheduling annotation, `@Scheduled(fixedRate = 1000L)`, to generate a new event every `1000` milliseconds. It uses Java's convenient `Random` utility class to rotate between three hostnames and all four severities.

> Why is the final case set to `default`? Java expects local variables to be initialized. If we replace `default` with the case limit value, then Java has no way of knowing that we covered all possible random values and would consider the value potentially uninitialized. Hence, it will throw an error about potentially not populating either `hostname` or `severity`.

We've coded an event simulator, that is, a producer. Now let's write an event consumer:

```
package learningspringboot;

import org.slf4j.Logger;
import org.slf4j.LoggerFactory;
import org.springframework.stereotype.Component;

@Component
public class NetworkEventConsumer {

    private static final Logger log =
            LoggerFactory.getLogger(NetworkEventConsumer.class);

    public void process(Alarm event) {
        log.info("Processing " + event);
    }
}
```

This is the entry point to our core business function: processing incoming events. In a real system, the `process` method will update the state of related devices, open tickets, and send alerts to regional operators. However, since this a demo, it simply logs the receipt of the event.

Do you see any hint of JMS? There is none to be found. There isn't any Spring except the `@Component` stereotype. This makes it possible for component scanning to pick this class up and add it to the application context.

All this component has is a simple method, `process`, that expects to be fed an `Alarm`. It merely logs the event and moves on. When we wire this into our app a little further down, we'll have created a **message-driven POJO**.

 So, what is the benefit of a message-driven POJO? Simple. With a POJO, we can easily write unit tests for our consumer logic. In this case, we would be testing the alarm correlation logic without the ceremony of containers, expensive startup sequences, or any other unforeseeable circumstances. Since the event correlation logic is decoupled from the message passing configuration, we also have the option to move from JMS to AMQP without having to alter the functionality.

The only thing left to do is wire up our app as follows:

```
package learningspringboot;

import javax.jms.ConnectionFactory;

import org.springframework.boot.SpringApplication;
import
org.springframework.boot.autoconfigure.EnableAutoConfiguration;
import org.springframework.context.annotation.Bean;
import org.springframework.context.annotation.ComponentScan;
import org.springframework.context.annotation.Configuration;
import org.springframework.jms.core.JmsTemplate;
import
org.springframework.jms.listener.SimpleMessageListenerContainer;
import
org.springframework.jms.listener.adapter.MessageListenerAdapter;
import org.springframework.scheduling.annotation.EnableScheduling;

@Configuration
@ComponentScan
@EnableScheduling
@EnableAutoConfiguration
public class Application {

    private static final String MAILBOX = "events";

    @Bean
    MessageListenerAdapter adapter(NetworkEventConsumer consumer) {
        MessageListenerAdapter adapter =
                new MessageListenerAdapter(consumer);
```

```
        adapter.setDefaultListenerMethod("process");
        return adapter;
    }

    @Bean
    SimpleMessageListenerContainer
    container(MessageListenerAdapter
            adapter, ConnectionFactory factory) {
        SimpleMessageListenerContainer container =
                new SimpleMessageListenerContainer();
        container.setMessageListener(adapter);
        container.setConnectionFactory(factory);
        container.setDestinationName(MAILBOX);
        return container;
    }

    @Bean
    NetworkEventSimulator simulator(JmsTemplate jmsTemplate) {
        return new NetworkEventSimulator(jmsTemplate, MAILBOX);
    }

    public static void main(String[] args) {
        SpringApplication.run(Application.class, args);
    }
}
```

Let's break this down:

- `@Configuration`: This looks for bean definitions inside the preceding class
- `@ComponentScan`: This looks for components, controllers, and other types in the preceding class's package to add to the application context
- `@EnableScheduling`: This turns on the simulator's `@Scheduled` event generator
- `@EnableAutoConfiguration`: This turns on Spring Boot's auto-configuration logic

The class contains the definitive name of our JMS destination, `events`.

There is a `MessageListenerAdapter` class. This convenient class lets us wrap any POJO so we can push events to it. In this case, we are wrapping `NetworkEventConsumer` and flagging its `process` method as the destination of JMS messages.

The `SimpleMessageListenerContainer` class is a super useful way to register the `MessageListenerAdapter` instance with the broker via the `ConnectionFactory` property. It also hooks things up to the `events` destination.

We can also see `NetworkEventSimulator` gets wired up by feeding it `JmsTemplate` and `MAILBOX`.

In addition to all this, we need a slight tweak to `build.gradle`. Sometimes, ActiveMQ can leave behind persistent data. By default, it ends up in `activemq-data` in the same folder from which the app runs. In order to have a clean slate for each start, we need to add this extra functionality when the `clean` task is invoked:

```
clean {
    delete "activemq-data"
}
```

Let's fire things up and see what happens!

```
$ ./gradlew clean bootRun

...

  .   ____          _            __ _ _
 /\\ / ___'_ __ _ _(_)_ __  __ _ \ \ \ \
( ( )\___ | '_ | '_| | '_ \/ _` | \ \ \ \
 \\/  ___)| |_)| | | | | || (_| |  ) ) ) )
  '  |____| .__|_| |_|_| |_\__, | / / / /
 =========|_|==============|___/=/_/_/_/
 :: Spring Boot ::        (v1.1.6.RELEASE)


2014-06-29 00:06:02.059 ... : Starting Application on retina with PID
16991 (/...
2014-06-29 00:06:02.113 ... : Refreshing org.springframework.context.
annotatio...
2014-06-29 00:06:02.655 ... : Bean 'org.springframework.scheduling.
annotation....
2014-06-29 00:06:02.951 ... : Using Persistence Adapter:
MemoryPersistenceAdap...
2014-06-29 00:06:02.953 ... : JMX consoles can connect to
service:jmx:rmi:///j...
2014-06-29 00:06:03.095 ... : Apache ActiveMQ 5.9.1 (localhost,
ID:retina-5395...
2014-06-29 00:06:03.099 ... : Apache ActiveMQ 5.9.1 (localhost,
ID:retina-5395...
```

```
2014-06-29 00:06:03.099 ... : For help or more information please see:
http://...
2014-06-29 00:06:03.128 ... : Connector vm://localhost started
2014-06-29 00:06:03.314 ... : Registering beans for JMX exposure on
startup
2014-06-29 00:06:03.329 ... : Starting beans in phase 2147483647
2014-06-29 00:06:03.337 ... : Started Application in 1.638 seconds (JVM
runnin...
2014-06-29 00:06:03.425 ... : Processing Event[switch1143:DEGRADED]
2014-06-29 00:06:04.342 ... : Processing Event[multiplex205:JEOPARDY]
2014-06-29 00:06:05.345 ... : Processing Event[multiplex205:JEOPARDY]
2014-06-29 00:06:06.343 ... : Processing Event[switch1143:UP]
2014-06-29 00:06:07.343 ... : Processing Event[router101:DEGRADED]
2014-06-29 00:06:08.345 ... : Processing Event[switch1143:DEGRADED]
2014-06-29 00:06:09.344 ... : Processing Event[router101:JEOPARDY]
```

So, what's happening? It might be slightly trimmed out of this text, but `Connector vm://localhost started` indicates that an embedded ActiveMQ broker was launched. It is listening to the virtual address `vm://localhost`. How did this happen? After all, we didn't code anything that involved setting up a broker.

Spring Boot kindly stepped in, thanks to `@EnableAutoConfiguration`. It saw that we had `spring-jms` and `activemq-broker` as dependencies. Both of these things caused Spring Boot to automatically configure and launch an embedded message broker.

Spring Boot also automatically created `JmsTemplate` and added this to the application context. This is how we were able to publish messages from `NetworkEventSimulator`. Also, we can see a random slew of events being processed in the preceding console output.

Sure, it's nice and handy to have what happened laid out in a book. However, what about the next app that we'll build? How are we going to deduce what Boot is doing? What if we use completely different modules? In the next few sections, we'll see exactly what Spring Boot does and why it does it. Armed with such knowledge, we'll be able to figure out what Boot will do in the future.

To get a handle on things, let's first see how Spring Boot auto-configured `JmsTemplate`. Here is a snippet of code from Spring Boot's JMS autodetection capabilities:

```
...
package org.springframework.boot.autoconfigure.jms;
...
/**
```

```
 * {@link EnableAutoConfiguration Auto-configuration} for Spring JMS.
 *
 * @author Greg Turnquist
 */
@Configuration
@ConditionalOnClass(JmsTemplate.class)
@ConditionalOnBean(ConnectionFactory.class)
@EnableConfigurationProperties(JmsProperties.class)
@AutoConfigureAfter({ HornetQAutoConfiguration.class,
ActiveMQAutoConfiguration.class })
public class JmsAutoConfiguration {

    @Autowired
    private JmsProperties properties;

    @Autowired
    private ConnectionFactory connectionFactory;

...
```

> This code isn't part of this book despite having my name on
> it. Instead, it's a feature I contributed to Spring Boot back in
> September of 2013 during the SpringOne conference.

Let's explore what this snippet of Spring Boot contains, which is as follows:

- @Configuration: This class contains beans to be added to the application context

- @ConditionOnClass: This class won't activate unless it detects JmsTemplate on the classpath (a tell-tale sign of spring-jms)

- @ConditionalOnBean: This class won't activate unless a bean exists of type javax.jms.ConnectionFactory

- @EnableConfigurationProperties: This class looks at JmsProperties for a set of property values

- @AutoConfigureAfter: Only do this one *after* checking HornetQ and ActiveMQ auto-configuration settings to avoid a configuration race condition

We can also see the autowired JmsProperties and ConnectionFactory.
Given all this, let's examine a core piece of this auto-configuration class:

```
@Bean
@ConditionalOnMissingBean
```

```
public JmsTemplate jmsTemplate() {
    JmsTemplate jmsTemplate = new
    JmsTemplate(this.connectionFactory);
    jmsTemplate.setPubSubDomain(this.properties.isPubSubDomain());
    return jmsTemplate;
}
```

This is a bean definition and runs only if there isn't already a `JmsTemplate` bean. This means that if we define our own bean, it won't kick in. This is how we can override Boot's opinion on how to configure this bean. It creates `JmsTemplate` using the autowired connection factory. Then it sets `pubSubDomain` based on the injected properties. Finally, it returns the template, loading it into the application context. That makes this bean available for us to wire into our application as shown earlier.

> Do I have to read Boot's source code every time I want to auto-configure something? Not really. The reference docs are quite thorough. Also, Boot makes some pretty good decisions that shouldn't surprise you. Appendix A of Boot's online reference manual (`http://docs.spring.io/spring-boot/docs/1.1.6.RELEASE/reference/htmlsingle/#common-application-properties`) contains an extensive listing of properties you can override, such as `spring.jms.*` and `spring.activemq.*`. However, the docs can't be guaranteed to always be right, nor can they necessarily document every single feature. Some third-party libraries are creating their own auto-configuration behaviors as well, with their own properties. See `https://github.com/codecentric/spring-boot-starter-batch-web` for an example. Understanding how Spring Boot does its auto-configuration is powerful knowledge, not only for using it, but also for potentially writing your own auto-configuration behaviors in the future.

Now that we've seen how Boot can auto-configure beans, let's explore the other tools Boot comes with.

Using Spring Boot's auto-configuration report

Spring Boot provides a very useful report to tip you off about what it's doing. There are different ways to turn on the report, shown as follows:

- Inside your IDE, add `--debug` as a program argument. Then run it.
- From the command line, execute `./gradlew clean build && java -jar build/libs/network-monitor-0.0.1-SNAPSHOT.jar --debug`.

If you try to put `--debug` into the `gradlew` command,
it will signal `gradlew` itself to generate a debug trail and
not get passed on to the app.

The results should look something like this:

```
=========================

AUTO-CONFIGURATION REPORT

=========================



Positive matches:

-----------------


  ActiveMQAutoConfiguration

    - @ConditionalOnClass classes found: javax.jms.
ConnectionFactory,org.apache.activemq.ActiveMQConnectionFactory
(OnClassCondition)

    - @ConditionalOnMissingBean (types: javax.jms.ConnectionFactory;
SearchStrategy: all) found no beans (OnBeanCondition)


  ActiveMQAutoConfiguration.EmbeddedBroker

    - Embedded ActiveMQ broker detected - brokerUrl 'vm://
localhost?broker.persistent=false' (ActiveMQAutoConfiguration.
EmbeddedBrokerCondition)

    - @ConditionalOnClass classes found: org.apache.activemq.transport.
vm.VMTransportFactory (OnClassCondition)


  JmsAutoConfiguration

    - @ConditionalOnClass classes found: org.springframework.jms.core.
JmsTemplate (OnClassCondition)

    - @ConditionalOnBean (types: javax.jms.ConnectionFactory;
SearchStrategy: all) found the following [jmsConnectionFactory]
(OnBeanCondition)


  JmsAutoConfiguration#jmsTemplate

    - @ConditionalOnMissingBean (types: org.springframework.jms.core.
JmsTemplate; SearchStrategy: all) found no beans (OnBeanCondition)

  ...
```

For space reasons, this snippet only shows a subset of **positive matches**. It is listing the auto-configuration code Spring Boot turned on. If you scroll further down when you execute this command, you'll also see a very long list of **negative matches**, which are things that Spring Boot did not activate.

From this preceding list, we can see what auto-configuration classes were activated:

Auto-configuration class	Quick description
ActiveMQAutoConfiguration	This is an enclosing auto-configuration for ActiveMQ
ActiveMQAutoConfiguration. EmbeddedBroker	This creates an embedded ActiveMQ broker
JmsAutoConfiguration	This is an enclosing auto-configuration for JMS
JmsAutoConfiguration#jmsTemplate	This creates JmsTemplate

 If you run this yourself, you'll find some other auto-configuration behaviors that were activated. However, since they are unrelated to JMS and ActiveMQ, they've been left out.

Auto-configuring ActiveMQ

Let's dive into the section of the report concerning ActiveMQAutoConfiguration:

```
@ConditionalOnClass classes found: javax.jms.ConnectionFactory,org.
apache.activemq.ActiveMQConnectionFactory (OnClassCondition)
```

This piece of the preceding report shows that ActiveMQAutoConfiguration and all its inner auto-configuration classes will be evaluated because it discovered ConnectionFactory and ActiveMQConnectionFactory on the classpath. Let's read some more:

```
@ConditionalOnMissingBean (types: javax.jms.ConnectionFactory;
SearchStrategy: all) found no beans (OnBeanCondition)
```

This bit of the report shows that Spring Boot also requires that no beans of type ConnectionFactory exist. This condition says that if we create a bean of this type, the entire ActiveMQAutoConfiguration will switch off.

 If we configure our own connection factory manually, there is little that Boot has to offer in automation and it's frankly too hard to line up property settings.

After `ActiveMQAutoConfiguration`, the report lists `ActiveMQAutoConfiguration.EmbeddedBroker`. The nomenclature of **<name>.<name>** says this is an inner class. Let's continue reading the report:

```
Embedded ActiveMQ broker detected - brokerUrl 'vm://localhost?broker.
persistent=false' (ActiveMQAutoConfiguration.EmbeddedBrokerCondition)
```

This is a custom condition. Most of the ones provided by Spring Boot are annotations (one exception is SpEL support). The message clearly says that it looked at the default URL (`vm://localhost`) and deduced this as the basis of an embedded broker. Let's look at some more of this report:

```
@ConditionalOnClass classes found: org.apache.activemq.transport.
vm.VMTransportFactory (OnClassCondition)
```

It also sees `VMTransportFactory` on the classpath. This class is only found in `activemq-broker`, indicating that we not only have the ActiveMQ client library, but also everything needed to run an embedded broker.

Making a change and debugging the results

What does the report look like if we switch our build file from `activemq-broker` to `activemq-client` and rerun everything?

It fails with the following message: `No qualifying bean of type [javax.jms.ConnectionFactory] found for dependency`. By itself, this might seem a bit confusing. After all, we were expecting Spring Boot to put together our connection factory. So, run the report again.

Earlier, we were only looking at positive matches. This time, `ActiveMQAutoConfiguration` has some results in negative matches:

```
ActiveMQAutoConfiguration.EmbeddedBroker

  - Embedded ActiveMQ broker detected - brokerUrl 'vm://localhost?broker.
persistent=false' (ActiveMQAutoConfiguration.EmbeddedBrokerCondition)

  - required @ConditionalOnClass classes not found: org.apache.activemq.
transport.vm.VMTransportFactory (OnClassCondition)


ActiveMQAutoConfiguration.NetworkBroker

  - Network ActiveMQ broker not detected - brokerUrl 'vm://
localhost?broker.persistent=false' (ActiveMQAutoConfiguration.
NonEmbeddedBrokerCondition)
```

Seeing both `EmbeddedBroker` and `NetworkBroker` listed indicates that Spring Boot could neither find an embedded broker nor a network broker. Why?

The EmbeddedBroker condition succeeds at detecting a URL starting with vm://, but fails because VMTransportFactory is no longer on the classpath. This is expected since we removed activemq-broker from the build.

Strangely, NetworkBroker fails as well. The Network ActiveMQ broker not detected - brokerUrl 'vm://localhost... message indicates that it didn't detect a network broker. Given that vm:// is the protocol for an embedded broker, it is apparent that this address is not suitable to use for connecting to a standalone broker. If we visit Boot's docs, we can find the ActiveMQ section (http://docs. spring.io/spring-boot/docs/1.1.6.RELEASE/reference/htmlsingle/#boot-features-activemq). From here, we can discover a hyperlink behind ActiveMQProperties that takes us to the source of spring.activemq properties. Here, we see that spring.activemq.inMemory defaults to true and requires an override to switch to using a network broker.

> Why does Boot require an override instead of switching to network broker mode? Because it can't discern our intent. There's simply not enough information. We either made a typo in the build file by not pulling in activemq-broker or we need to explicitly tell it to switch to network mode. Either way, we need to clarify our intent to Boot.

Let's add the following line to src/main/resources/application.properties:

```
spring.activemq.inMemory=false
```

This says not to use in-memory settings. Given this, Spring Boot now has enough information to create a connection factory. So, let's rerun our app once more.

It fails again, but for a different reason: Could not connect to broker URL: tcp://localhost:61616. This sounds more reasonable because we never stood up a broker.

We now see this in positive matches in the auto-configuration report:

```
ActiveMQAutoConfiguration.NetworkBroker

  - Network ActiveMQ broker detected - brokerUrl 'tcp://localhost:61616'
(ActiveMQAutoConfiguration.NonEmbeddedBrokerCondition)
```

It recognizes that tcp:// is the protocol for a remote and standalone broker on the default port. Additionally, ActiveMQAutoConfiguration.EmbeddedBroker is in negative matches, as it should be. It indicates that the only thing needed is to configure an ActiveMQ server.

We can either download ActiveMQ or install it through any popular package manager. On a Mac with Homebrew, we only have to run the following commands:

```
$ brew install activemq
$ activemq start
```

Run the app and it should now start cranking out network events such as we saw at the beginning of this chapter. (By the way, don't forget to shut down your broker by typing activemq stop when you're done.)

Whenever we see one of these auto-configuration classes, we can easily Google the name of the class and it will lead us to the source code. Or we can open it up inside our IDE and ask it to fetch the source. Given all the tools we've looked at so far, we have the building blocks to reach beyond the reference docs and see how Spring Boot is configuring things.

Overriding Boot with alternate beans or properties

This section assumes that you have reverted your build file back to using activemq-broker and removed spring.activemq.inMemory=false, hence going back to the in-memory embedded ActiveMQ broker.

In the previous section, we saw how Spring Boot inserts its opinion when it sees spring-jms on the path. It distinctly creates JmsTemplate. But , what if we don't like its opinion?

The jmsTemplate method inside JmsAutoConfiguration was flagged with @ConditionalOnMissingBean. This means that if we create our own bean definition for JmsTemplate, Spring Boot will back off and instead let us plug in our own bean.

JMS supports two types of message destinations: **queues** and **topics**. By default, JmsTemplate is configured to talk to queues. To reconfigure it to talk to topics requires a change in the bean definition. Let's add our own bean to Application.java:

```
@Bean
JmsTemplate jmsTemplate(ConnectionFactory factory) {
    JmsTemplate jmsTemplate = new JmsTemplate(factory);
    jmsTemplate.setPubSubDomain(true);
    return jmsTemplate;
}
```

Let's walk through this code:

- The `@Bean` annotation indicates that this is a bean definition.
- A `ConnectionFactory` instance is required. If one doesn't exist, the app will fail quickly.
- A `JmsTemplate` instance is created and its `pubSubDomain` property is set to `true`.
- The object is returned.

If the publisher is talking to topics with this instance of `JmsTemplate`, the consumer must be configured as the same. Check out the following update to `SimpleMessageListenerContainer`:

```
@Bean
SimpleMessageListenerContainer container(MessageListenerAdapter adapter,
        ConnectionFactory factory) {
    SimpleMessageListenerContainer container =
            new SimpleMessageListenerContainer();
    container.setMessageListener(adapter);
    container.setConnectionFactory(factory);
    container.setPubSubDomain(true);
    container.setDestinationName(MAILBOX);
    return container;
}
```

The preceding code is the same as seen earlier except that `container.setPubSubDomain(true)` has been added to make it listen to topics.

> What is the significance of queues versus topics? Queues are one-to-one. Topics are one-to-many. In either paradigm, multiple publishers can send messages to multiple consumers through a single destination. The difference is that with a queue, only one of the consumers will get any given message. With a topic, all the consumers will get a copy (barring any message selectors).

It's really handy to be able to swap out Boot's `JmsTemplate` class for our own. Doesn't that seem a bit heavyweight just to override a single property? Thankfully, lots of Boot's auto-configurations are loaded with property settings. This gives us more fine-grained control over things.

First, we can throw out that custom `JmsTemplate` bean definition. Then, we only need to create `src/main/resources/application.properties` and add this:

```
spring.jms.pubSubDomain=true
```

This property will set Boot's `JmsTemplate.pubSubDomain` field to `true`.

We still have to alter our `SimpleMessageListenerContainer` configuration to follow suit. We can go in and hardcode the container's `pubSubDomain` property, but doesn't that sound a bit inflexible? Wouldn't it be better if we hooked into Spring Boot's property settings directly? This way, if the property is updated anywhere, either in `application.properties` or via the other options mentioned previously in this book after our code is released, our code will keep up with the changes.

To do this, we need our own copy of `JmsProperties` injected into `Application.java`:

```
@Autowired
private JmsProperties properties;
```

 Remember, `JmsProperties` is the source of properties that were mentioned earlier.

What does this code mean? Spring's `@Autowired` annotation will ensure that we get a copy of the same `JmsProperties` bean created by Spring Boot.

With this in place, we can update our bean definition of `SimpleMessageListenerContainer` as follows:

```
@Bean
SimpleMessageListenerContainer container(MessageListenerAdapter consumer,
                                          ConnectionFactory factory) {
    SimpleMessageListenerContainer container =
            new SimpleMessageListenerContainer();
    container.setMessageListener(consumer);
    container.setConnectionFactory(factory);
    container.setPubSubDomain(this.properties.isPubSubDomain());
    container.setDestinationName(MAILBOX);
    return container;
}
```

The `container.setPubSubDomain(this.properties.isPubSubDomain())` statement sets the container's `pubSubDomain` field based on the property. In *Chapter 2, Quick Start with Java*, we briefly mentioned Spring Boot's various options to configure properties. To summarize:

- Default values can be supplied directly as `@Value("${propertyName: defaultValue}")`

- The `@Value` annotation defaults can be overridden in an `application.properties` file, which gets bundled with the app in a JAR file

- Bundled properties can be overridden in an auxiliary `application.properties` file adjacent to the deployed JAR file

- Auxiliary properties can be overridden with environment variables, either from the command line, `.bashrc`, or Windows environment settings

- In a cloud environment, environment variables can be supplied by other means we won't delve into

Our app is now configured to use topics. If we run it from our IDE, we can expect to see something like this:

```
  .   ____          _            __ _ _
 /\\ / ___'_ __ _ _(_)_ __  __ _ \ \ \ \
( ( )\___ | '_ | '_| | '_ \/ _` | \ \ \ \
 \\/  ___)| |_)| | | | | || (_| |  ) ) ) )
  '  |____| .__|_| |_|_| |_\__, | / / / /
 =========|_|==============|___/=/_/_/_/
 :: Spring Boot ::        (v1.1.6.RELEASE)


2014-07-05 01:28:10.651 ... : Starting Application on retina with PID
30378 (/...
2014-07-05 01:28:10.695 ... : Refreshing org.springframework.context.
annotatio...
2014-07-05 01:28:11.206 ... : Bean 'org.springframework.scheduling.
annotation....
2014-07-05 01:28:11.508 ... : Using Persistence Adapter:
MemoryPersistenceAdap...
2014-07-05 01:28:11.512 ... : JMX consoles can connect to
service:jmx:rmi:///j...
2014-07-05 01:28:11.656 ... : Apache ActiveMQ 5.9.1 (localhost,
ID:retina-5625...
```

```
2014-07-05 01:28:11.661 ... : Apache ActiveMQ 5.9.1 (localhost,
ID:retina-5625...

2014-07-05 01:28:11.661 ... : For help or more information please see:
http://...

2014-07-05 01:28:11.697 ... : Connector vm://localhost started

2014-07-05 01:28:11.850 ... : Registering beans for JMX exposure on
startup

2014-07-05 01:28:11.867 ... : Starting beans in phase 2147483647

2014-07-05 01:28:11.875 ... : Started Application in 1.564 seconds (JVM
runnin...

2014-07-05 01:28:11.950 ... : Processing Event[switch1143:DOWN]

2014-07-05 01:28:12.881 ... : Processing Event[switch1143:UP]

2014-07-05 01:28:13.883 ... : Processing Event[switch1143:DOWN]

2014-07-05 01:28:14.882 ... : Processing Event[switch1143:UP]

2014-07-05 01:28:15.883 ... : Processing Event[router101:DOWN]

2014-07-05 01:28:16.880 ... : Processing Event[switch1143:UP]

2014-07-05 01:28:17.880 ... : Processing Event[switch1143:JEOPARDY]
```

 We are just exploring a single JMS property. For a guide to common application properties provided by Spring Boot, read http://docs. spring.io/spring-boot/docs/1.1.6.RELEASE/reference/ htmlsingle/#common-application-properties.

Writing a custom health check to ping ActiveMQ

We've gotten a glimpse of how Spring Boot does auto-configuration, and we've also seen how to tap Boot's property support. In previous chapters, we saw how Spring Boot comes with additional ops-ready support via its **Actuator** module. Let's turn that on and customize the health indicator to also ping the ActiveMQ broker.

First, we need to add key dependencies to build.gradle to make these HTTP management endpoints visible:

```
compile("org.springframework.boot:spring-boot-actuator")
compile("org.springframework.boot:spring-boot-starter-web")
```

What do we have here? The `spring-boot-actuator` module is the key module to add these various management services. But these endpoints also require Spring MVC. Since the app we've developed so far has not involved any client layer, we also need to add the `spring-boot-starter-web` module.

 We've been using `spring-boot-starter-thymeleaf` in the previous chapters. The data served up from Actuator doesn't actually use views, but instead returns data in a JSON structure.

If we launch the app with `./gradlew bootRun` and visit `http://localhost:8080/health`, we will see the following output:

This shows a simple **UP** message. What does this indicate? Well, Spring Boot has `ApplicationHealthIndicator`, which is hardcoded to return **UP**. It basically indicates whether or not the app is running.

Something more meaningful for our app will be to ping the ActiveMQ message broker. How can we do that? Look at the following code:

```
package learningspringboot;

import javax.jms.ConnectionFactory;
import javax.jms.JMSException;

import org.springframework.beans.factory.annotation.Autowired;
import org.springframework.boot.actuate.health.Health;
import org.springframework.boot.actuate.health.HealthIndicator;
import org.springframework.boot.actuate.health.Status;
import org.springframework.stereotype.Component;
```

```
@Component
public class ActiveMQHealth implements HealthIndicator {

    private ConnectionFactory factory;

    @Autowired
    public ActiveMQHealth(ConnectionFactory factory) {
        this.factory = factory;
    }

    @Override
    public Health health() {
        try {
            factory.createConnection();
        } catch (JMSException e) {
            return new Health.Builder()
                    .down(e)
                    .build();
        }
        return new Health.Builder()
                .status(Status.UP + ": Successfully connected to
                the broker")
                .build();
    }
}
```

Let's walk through the bits and pieces of the preceding code snippet:

- The `@Component` annotation flags this class to be picked up by `@ComponentScan`.

- It implements Actuator's `HealthIndicator` interface so it can be scooped up automatically.

- It gets `ConnectionFactory` autowired by constructor.

- Inside `health()`, it tries to create a connection. If it fails, that is, throws an exception, a **DOWN** status is returned along with the exception.

- If the connection is created, it returns **UP** with a more detailed message about reaching the broker.

 The `ConnectionFactory` instance is wired via constructor injection. For more information, read `http://docs.spring.io/spring/docs/4.0.7.RELEASE/spring-framework-reference/htmlsingle/#beans-dependency-resolution`.

Launch the app and visit `http://localhost:8080/health` once again, and we will get the following output:

Here, we can see our new health status message, clearly indicating that it was able to hit the broker.

This idea is pretty handy. In this chapter, we have already seen how easy it is to either fetch key beans or look up property values. This makes it easy to write a health indicator that can tap database credentials or perhaps a REST service URL to test that critical components are up.

To top things off, Spring Boot Actuator comes with several built-in health checks based on the current environment. For example, it will do extra checks against MongoDB, Redis, RabbitMQ, Solr, and any DataSource-based DB to check whether they're up and include them in the `/health` management endpoint.

Adding customized app data to /info

If you added Spring Boot's Actuator module to a given project, another endpoint is available: `/info`. This endpoint actually returns the empty JSON document { }. This isn't very useful. Never fear because Spring Boot makes it super simple to embed whatever you want.

Any property that starts with `info.` will be scooped up and served from this endpoint. Let's add the following code to `src/main/resources/application.properties`:

```
info.app.name=Network Manager
info.app.project=Learning Spring Boot
```

```
info.app.chapter=3
info.app.manuscript.raw=asciidoctor
info.app.manuscript.formatted=LibreOffice
info.app.manuscript.converter=https://github.com/gregturn/asciidoc
tor-packt
```

 There is no fixed structure to this. You only have to start with `info`.

Interesting material to serve up, but we can do better. Have you ever deployed a system only to have a customer call you up and complain, "The app is broken!" Through a handful of questions, you discover the issue is something you already fixed and rolled out. After a few hours of painstaking research, you figure out that they are using the previous version! What would have been handy is precise version information. What would be more precise than having access to a commit ID? This way, we can ask our customer over the phone exactly what version they have and quickly rule out issues.

What will be handy is embedding information from the build process into `application.properties`. To do so, we must add the following fragment to `build.gradle`:

```
import org.apache.tools.ant.filters.*

afterEvaluate {
    configure(allProcessResourcesTasks()) {
        filter(ReplaceTokens,
            tokens: [baseName: project.jar.baseName,
                     version: project.jar.version,
                     gradleVersion: project.gradle.gradleVersion]
        )
    }
}

def allProcessResourcesTasks() {
    sourceSets*.processResourcesTaskName.collect {
        tasks[it]
    }
}
```

This fragment of Gradle code will find various property files. Then it will try to replace any existing tokens found in the form of `@some-property@` with the list of items in `tokens`.

Therefore, we can add the following properties to `application.properties` to grant us extra information about the build:

```
info.build.artifact=@baseName@
info.build.version=@version@
info.build.gradleVersion=@gradleVersion@
```

These properties will be replaced by the ones defined in `tokens`, as shown earlier. It will provide us with the following items in the browser:

- The name of the artifact
- The version number of the artifact
- The version of gradle used to build the app

On top of that, if we are using Git (like the source code of this book), we can use the gradle-git plugin (`https://github.com/ajoberstar/gradle-git`) to fetch commit details and use it to produce `git.properties`. Whenever Spring Boot Actuator spots such a file, it automatically serves up its properties as additional information underneath `/info`.

For starters, we need to add this fragment to `build.gradle` as well:

```
import org.ajoberstar.grgit.*

configure(rootProject) {
    task gitMetadata << {
        ext {
            repo = Grgit.open(project.file('../..'))
            branch = repo.branch?.current?.name
            commitId = repo.head().abbreviatedId
            commitTime = new Date(new Integer(repo.head().time)
                    .longValue()*1000L).format("yyyy-MM-dd HH:mm")
        }
    }

    apply from: 'writeGitPropertiesFile.gradle'
}
```

What does the preceding fragment of Gradle configuration do?

- The `configure` method applies extra configuration steps to `rootProject`, which represents the entire project. (It's possible to apply subsections of a project, but we aren't diving into that.)

- It declares a task named `gitMetadata`, which outputs a handful of properties.

- To fetch Git properties, the `Grgit` module first opens the Git repository using `Grgit.open(project.file('../..'))`. This command looks up two parent folders because that is the structure of this book's manuscript. For a standard project, you should probably use `Grgit.open(project.file('.'))`.

- Then it looks up the branch's current name, the head commit's abbreviated ID (the first seven characters of the full ID), and the head commit's time (formatted to be human readable).

- Finally, it imports another Gradle build file, `writeGitPropertiesFile.gradle`, put in the same folder as `build.gradle`.

So, let's look at the `writeGitPropertiesFiles.gradle` file:

```
task writeGitPropertiesFile(dependsOn: [ rootProject.gitMetadata,
processResources ]) {
    ext.outputFile = file("${sourceSets.main.
    output.resourcesDir}/git.properties")

    doLast() {
        new Properties(
                'git.branch' : gitMetadata.branch,
                'git.commit.id' : gitMetadata.commitId,
                'git.commit.time' : gitMetadata.commitTime
        ).store(new BufferedWriter(new FileWriter(outputFile)) {
            public void write(String s, int off, int len) throws
            IOException {
                if (s.startsWith("#")) {
                    return
                }
                super.write(s, off, len)
            }
        }, null)
    }
}
jar.inputs.file writeGitPropertiesFile.outputFile
jar.dependsOn writeGitPropertiesFile
```

This file defines another task aimed at writing all this Git metadata to `git.properties`. Let's break it down:

- This task declares a dependency on `rootProject.gitMetadata`, which we just finished explaining.

- Then it declares the output file to be {`sourceSets.main.output.resourcesDir`}/`git.properties`, which is essentially the folder all `src/main/resource` files are copied into before JARing them up.

- Next, it constructs a Java `Properties` object and loads it with property names and values, read from `gitMetadata`. This is written to disk using `BufferedWriter`.

- As a last step, the task tells the project's `jar` task that this task's output file (`git.properties`) should be included as both an input and a dependency. This ensures that the JAR command doesn't run before this phase is executed.

> Remember, this mechanism of fetching project and Git properties is only available if we are using gradle as our build tool. To do similar things with Maven, see http://docs.spring.io/spring-boot/docs/1.1.6.RELEASE/reference/htmlsingle/#production-ready-application-info. Also, these are only available when using a runnable JAR file, not from `bootRun`.

Now, let's bundle it up and run it:

```
$ ./gradlew clean build && java -jar build/libs/network-monitor-0.0.1-SNAPSHOT.jar
```

After the app is up, we can now visit http://localhost:8080/info and see the fruit of our efforts, which is as follows:

```
{
  - app: {
      chapter: "3",
    - manuscript: {
        raw: "asciidoctor",
        converter: "https://github.com/gregturn/asciidoctor-packt",
        formatted: "LibreOffice"
      },
      name: "Network Manager",
      project: "Learning Spring Boot"
    },
  - build: {
      artifact: "network-monitor",
      description: "Learning Spring Boot",
      group: "learningspringboot",
      version: "0.0.1-SNAPSHOT"
    },
  - git: {
      branch: "master",
    - commit: {
        id: "3f83a5f",
        time: "2014-07-05T23:23:05-0500"
      }
    }
}
```

Spring Boot nicely breaks up the property names separated by dots into a hierarchical structure. The `build` section has information conveniently inserted from `build.gradle`. Also, `git` contains the branch name, commit hash ID, and time of the commit. Now when we get that 2:00 a.m. phone call, we can ask them to e-mail us a screenshot. Then we can quickly check it against our source repository and start solving the problem using the correct baseline.

> This mechanism of gathering properties and Git info to serve up underneath `/info` only works when we create and run the JAR file. Simply running the app from our IDE or using `./gradlew bootRun` won't produce any new content. It should also be pointed out that if we previously built a JAR file, that information will be served up even if it's stale.

Creating custom metrics to track the message traffic

We've created a custom health check and also added custom info about our app. Another useful strategy will be to create some custom metrics. In previous chapters, we saw how Spring Boot's Actuator comes with some out-of-the-box counters and gauges for web activity. For this section, let's count the flow of messages through the system.

Earlier in this chapter, we coded a simulator that would generate events periodically. The following fragment shows an updated version of that constructor to support metrics:

```
final private JmsTemplate jmsTemplate;
final private String destination;
final private CounterService counterService;

public NetworkEventSimulator(JmsTemplate jmsTemplate, String destination,
                            CounterService counterService) {
    this.jmsTemplate = jmsTemplate;
    this.destination = destination;
    this.counterService = counterService;
}
```

This constructor adds Spring Boot's `org.springframework.boot.actuate.metrics.CounterService` to the simulator, giving us the means to start counting generated events.

The following code shows more edits to the simulator:

```
@Scheduled(fixedRate = 1000L)
public void simulateActivity() {
    ...
    Alarm event = new Alarm(hostname, LocalDateTime.now(),
            severity);
    jmsTemplate.convertAndSend(destination, event);
    counterService.increment("messages.total.produced");
    counterService.increment("messages." + event.getHostname() +
    ".produced");
}
```

At the bottom of the `simulateActivity` method, we have added two extra lines after sending out the message. It increments two counters:

- `messages.total.produced`: This counts all messages

- `message.<hostname>.produced`: This counts messages split up by hostname

Now, let's edit `NetworkEventConsumer` as well:

```
package learningspringboot;

import org.slf4j.Logger;
import org.slf4j.LoggerFactory;
import org.springframework.beans.factory.annotation.Autowired;
import org.springframework.boot.actuate.metrics.CounterService;
import org.springframework.stereotype.Component;

@Component
public class NetworkEventConsumer {

    private static final Logger log =
            LoggerFactory.getLogger(NetworkEventConsumer.class);

    private final CounterService counterService;

    @Autowired
    public NetworkEventConsumer(CounterService counterService) {
        this.counterService = counterService;
    }

    public void process(Alarm event) {
        log.info("Processing " + event);
        counterService.increment("messages.total.consumed");
        counterService.increment("messages." + event.getHostname()
        + ".consumed");
    }
}
```

Here we do the same thing and populate `CounterService` by constructor injection. As we process messages, we are creating a metric similar to the simulator, only this time we are counting the messages consumed.

No further edits are necessary for `NetworkEventConsumer` because it's automatically loaded up by `@ComponentScan`. However, the `NetworkEventSimulator` class is wired up in `Application`, so we need to make edits there as well:

```
@Bean
NetworkEventSimulator simulator(JmsTemplate jmsTemplate,
CounterService counterService) {
    return new NetworkEventSimulator(jmsTemplate, MAILBOX,
    counterService);
}
```

This change in the `simulator` bean definition shows a `CounterService` instance fetched from the application context and injected into `NetworkEventSimulator` upon creation. Spring Boot Actuator automatically created this bean and added it to the application context, making it incredibly easy to tap into its metrics gathering system.

Now, when we run our app and visit `http://localhost:8080/metrics`, we should see something like the following screenshot:

Looking at the metrics, we can see the following:

- There have been 17 `multiplex205` messages produced and consumed
- There have been 20 `router101` messages produced and consumed
- There have been 15 `switch1143` messages produced and consumed
- This adds up to 52 total messages produced and consumed

We can also decrement counters. To top it off, Spring Boot Actuator also has a `GaugeService` that takes snapshot values in time that can capture anything. This opens the door to creating our own metrics, allowing us to track virtually anything. We can count errors, exceptions, and other bad behavior in our app.

Tweaking management ports, address, and paths

So far, we've done some debugging as well as customizing the metrics. Another valuable feature is how we can customize the management endpoints to our liking.

By default, the management endpoints (such as `/info` and `/metrics`) are simply different routes hosted on the same port. Let's change this from port `8080` to `9000` by adding this to `application.properties`:

```
management.port=9000
```

It's also possible to change the IP address that the management endpoints are hosted on, as follows:

```
management.address=127.0.0.1
```

This ensures that the management endpoints are only available when browsing on the machine itself. An alternative strategy would be to have the main application advertising itself on a public facing IP address while `management.address` is configured with a private, VPN-based address.

Also, what if we prefer to group all the endpoints under one path? We can tweak things like this:

```
management.context-path=/manage
```

Finally, it's good to know that each endpoint's route can be altered as well. To change the `info` endpoint, include the following code in `application.properties`:

```
endpoints.info.id=appdata
```

 The other endpoints you can adjust are `autoconfig`, `beans`, `configprops`, `dump`, `env`, `health`, `metrics`, `mappings`, `shutdown`, and `trace`. endpoints. The `<name>.id=/<newpath>` statement is the way to override the default routes.

So what happens if we visit the app through a public-facing site?

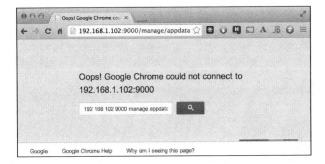

We can't see it! There is no unauthorized access or fancy error page. Instead, we simply have the browser telling us that such a path doesn't exist. We can't even deduce that this is a Spring Boot application because no information is given away.

 Want to test this out on your own machine? You probably won't have the same IP address shown on the screen. Try `ifconfig` or `ipconfig` and look for an address other than localhost or 127.0.0.1.

Now, let's visit the endpoint on localhost:

```
{
  - app: {
      - manuscript: {
            raw: "asciidoctor",
            formatted: "LibreOffice",
            converter: "https://github.com/gregturn/asciidoctor-packt"
        },
        name: "Network Manager",
        chapter: "3",
        project: "Learning Spring Boot"
    },
  - build: {
        description: "Learning Spring Boot",
        group: "learningspringboot",
        version: "0.0.1-SNAPSHOT",
        artifact: "network-monitor"
    },
  - git: {
        branch: "master",
      - commit: {
            id: "7edfbbf",
            time: "2014-07-07T00:32:33-0500"
        }
    }
}
```

We can see it now.

 Changing the port and the context path is arguably redundant. Setting a custom context path is meant to avoid conflicts with any existing routes. The same isolation is provided by changing management endpoints to a different port. We just combined these options together for demonstration purposes.

Restricting access only to JMX

We've created several customized endpoints and tailored things to suit our needs. But what if we prefer to do all the management work through JMX? We can easily shutdown HTTP endpoints if that's our planned configuration.

Let's replace the HTTP customizations in `application.properties` from the previous section with the following line:

```
management.port=-1
```

By setting the management port to -1, Spring Boot gets the message to switch off HTTP endpoints. Launch the application and there will be no Spring MVC management endpoints:

```
$ ./gradlew bootRun
...

  .   ____          _            __ _ _
 /\\ / ___'_ __ _ _(_)_ __  __ _ \ \ \ \
( ( )\___ | '_ | '_| | '_ \/ _` | \ \ \ \
 \\/  ___)| |_)| | | | | || (_| |  ) ) ) )
  '  |____| .__|_| |_|_| |_\__, | / / / /
 =========|_|==============|___/=/_/_/_/
 :: Spring Boot ::        (v1.1.6.RELEASE)


2014-07-11 22:26:19.194 ... : Starting Application on retina with PID 18850 (/...
...
2014-07-11 22:26:21.557 ... : JMX consoles can connect to service:jmx:rmi:///j...
...
```

```
2014-07-11 22:26:22.477 ... : Located managed bean
'requestMappingEndpoint': r...

2014-07-11 22:26:22.501 ... : Located managed bean 'environmentEndpoint':
regi...

2014-07-11 22:26:22.506 ... : Located managed bean 'healthEndpoint':
registeri...

2014-07-11 22:26:22.510 ... : Located managed bean 'beansEndpoint':
registerin...

2014-07-11 22:26:22.514 ... : Located managed bean 'infoEndpoint':
registering...

2014-07-11 22:26:22.519 ... : Located managed bean 'metricsEndpoint':
register...

2014-07-11 22:26:22.523 ... : Located managed bean 'traceEndpoint':
registerin...

2014-07-11 22:26:22.527 ... : Located managed bean 'dumpEndpoint':
registering...

2014-07-11 22:26:22.532 ... : Located managed bean
'autoConfigurationAuditEndp...

2014-07-11 22:26:22.535 ... : Located managed bean 'shutdownEndpoint':
registe...

2014-07-11 22:26:22.543 ... : Located managed bean
'configurationPropertiesRep...

2014-07-11 22:26:22.546 ... : Starting beans in phase 2147483647

2014-07-11 22:26:22.602 ... : Tomcat started on port(s): 8080/http

2014-07-11 22:26:22.604 ... : Started Application in 3.75 seconds (JVM
running...

...
```

Various beans such as infoEndpoint are shown in the preceding console output. However, these aren't the Spring MVC routes we saw earlier. Instead, it's the service beans that back them and they're being exposed as managed beans. If you run the code yourself, you will see more details, such as [org.springframework.boot: type=Endpoint,name=infoEndpoint].

Connecting to the app via JConsole and jmxterm

We can connect via JMX and interrogate them for information. There are multiple tools available, so why not start with JConsole, the one that comes with the JDK already on our system?

In one shell, we need to launch our application as follows:

```
$ ./gradlew bootRun
```

```
...
```

Somewhere in this console output, there is a debug message containing **JMX consoles can connect to service:jmx:rmi:///jndi/rmi://localhost:1099/jmxrmi**. Let's save this value so that we can use it further down in this section.

From another shell, launch JConsole as follows:

```
$ jconsole
```

A subwindow should pop up. Select **Remote Process** and enter the address we just found, as shown in the following screenshot:

With the connection string entered, we can click on **Connect** to attach to the application.

It's common to see another popup after this, reporting a failure to create a secure connection. If so, simply click on **Insecure** and it will switch to making an open, non-SSL-based connection.

Now if we navigate to **MBeans** and expand **org.springframework.boot** followed by **Endpoint**, we can see all the managed beans, as shown in the following screenshot:

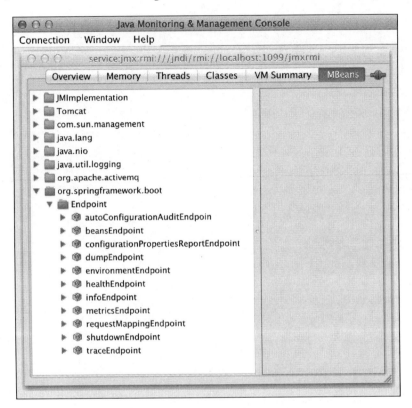

We can see the same data presented earlier from /info. Simply expand **infoEndpoint | Attributes | Data**:

```
app={chapter=3, manuscript={raw=asciidoctor, converter=https://github.
com/gregturn/asciidoctor-packt, formatted=LibreOffice}, name=Network
Manager, project=Learning Spring Boot}
build={artifact=${project.artifactId}, description=${project.
description}, group=${project.groupId}, version=${project.version}}
git={branch=master, commit={id=6b68107, time=2014-07-
08T22:49:24-0500}}
```

This is, again, the compressed version of data that might be difficult to parse. If we copy it to a text editor or our IDE, we might be able to reformat it to view.

Of course, JConsole isn't the only tool to access data served over JMX. A handy command-line tool, jmxterm (`http://wiki.cyclopsgroup.org/jmxterm/download.html`), can be used as well. Assuming we downloaded jmxterm (which is a runnable JAR file), we can proceed like this:

```
$ java -jar jmxterm-1.0-alpha-4-uber.jar --url service:jmx:rmi:///jndi/
rmi://localhost:1099/jmxrmi
Welcome to JMX terminal. Type "help" for available commands.
```

There are lots of beans, but we are only interested in the ones inside domain `org.springframework.boot`. Let's pick this domain and see what beans it contains:

```
$>domain org.springframework.boot
#domain is set to org.springframework.boot
$>beans
#domain = org.springframework.boot:
org.springframework.boot:name=autoConfigurationAuditEndpoint,
type=Endpoint
org.springframework.boot:name=beansEndpoint,type=Endpoint
org.springframework.boot:name=configurationPropertiesReportEndpoint,type=
Endpoint
org.springframework.boot:name=dumpEndpoint,type=Endpoint
org.springframework.boot:name=environmentEndpoint,type=Endpoint
org.springframework.boot:name=healthEndpoint,type=Endpoint
org.springframework.boot:name=infoEndpoint,type=Endpoint
org.springframework.boot:name=metricsEndpoint,type=Endpoint
org.springframework.boot:name=requestMappingEndpoint,type=Endpoint
org.springframework.boot:name=shutdownEndpoint,type=Endpoint
org.springframework.boot:name=traceEndpoint,type=Endpoint
```

This listing shows us all the management beans that are available.

Let's continue to check out `infoEndpoint` by picking it as our bean:

```
$>bean org.springframework.boot:name=infoEndpoint,type=Endpoint
#bean is set to org.springframework.boot:name=infoEndpoint,type=Endpoint
```

Let's see all the various attributes, operations, and notifications this endpoint has:

```
$>info
#mbean = org.springframework.boot:name=infoEndpoint,type=Endpoint
#class name = org.springframework.boot.actuate.endpoint.jmx.
DataEndpointMBean
# attributes
   %0    - Data (java.lang.Object, r)
   %1    - EndpointClass (java.lang.String, r)
   %2    - Sensitive (boolean, r)
# operations
   %0    - java.lang.Object getData()
   %1    - java.lang.String getEndpointClass()
   %2    - boolean isSensitive()
#there's no notifications
```

We can see three pieces of information: `Data`, `EndpointClass`, and `Sensitive`.

Let's fetch the `Data` attribute as follows:

```
$>get Data
#mbean = org.springframework.boot:name=infoEndpoint,type=Endpoint:
Data = {
  app = {
    chapter = 3;
    manuscript = {
      raw = asciidoctor;
      converter = https://github.com/gregturn/asciidoctor-packt;
      formatted = LibreOffice;
    };
    name = Network Manager;
    project = Learning Spring Boot;
  };
  build = {
    artifact = ${project.artifactId};
    description = ${project.description};
    group = ${project.groupId};
```

```
    version = ${project.version};
  };
  git = {
    branch = master;
    commit = {
      id = 6b68107;
      time = 2014-07-08T22:49:24-0500;
    };
  };
};
$>quit
```

This format is a bit nicer than what we saw inside JConsole. Also, feel free to look at the other bits of data tied to this endpoint. Visit the other endpoints as well and see what they have.

While the format inside jmxterm was nicer, navigating to the data was more unwieldy. Of course, JMX is a well-defined standard. We can either look for other tools or potentially write our own Java code to access these attributes. (Spring Boot CLI app perhaps?) Either way, JMX provides an alternative mechanism to access management data.

Creating custom CRaSH commands

In *Chapter 1, Quick Start with Groovy*, we got an initial glimpse of CRaSH (http://www.crashub.org/), the shell for Java apps. We took a quick tour of that application. In this section, we'll not only add CRaSH, but also write some custom commands.

First, we need to add `spring-boot-starter-remote-shell` to the build file:

```
compile("org.springframework.boot:spring-boot-starter-remote-
shell")
```

Now when we run our app, we will have a lot of out-of-the-box management features. However, the focus of this section is to create some custom commands and then see them in action.

Spring Boot Actuator will look in `classpath*:/commands/` and `classpath*:/crash/commands/` for any Groovy scripts. Let's write one!

Create `src/main/resources/commands/activemq.groovy` and start adding some key import statements at the top as follows:

```
package learningspringboot.commands

import org.crsh.cli.Command
import org.crsh.cli.Man
import org.crsh.cli.Usage
import org.crsh.command.InvocationContext
import org.springframework.beans.factory.BeanFactory
import org.springframework.boot.actuate.metrics.repository.
MetricRepository

import javax.jms.ConnectionFactory
```

> While the script is in `src/main/resources/commands`, there is no requirement for it to be in the `commands` package. So we've declared it to be nicely segmented into the `learningspringboot.commands` package.

Now let's start crafting some CRaSH commands. We'll start by coding the class declaration and the first method shown as follows:

```
...
@Usage("Various commands to interact with ActiveMQ JMS broker")
class activemq {

    @Usage("Check ActiveMQ status")
    @Man("Creates a connection to the broker. If successful,
    report 'UP'. If not, report 'DOWN'")
    @Command
    def ping(InvocationContext context) {
        BeanFactory beanFactory =
        context.attributes['spring.beanfactory']
        try {
            beanFactory.getBean(ConnectionFactory).
            createConnection()
            "Broker is UP!"
        } catch (JMSException) {
            "Broker is DOWN!"
        }
    }
...
```

There are quite a few aspects shown here. Let's walk through it line-by-line to understand how Spring Boot Actuator and CRaSH work together.

The `@Usage` annotation at the class level contains the description of our `activemq` command grouping. It will be shown when we type `help` inside CRaSH (as we'll see later in this section).

The class name itself, `activemq`, becomes part of what we'll type in the shell to invoke one of our commands. For this reason, we don't follow standard camel-case conventions and instead make it lowercase.

Each preceding method has a set of annotations described as follows:

- The `@Usage` annotation on the method provides a short description of the command when we type `activemq` and all commands are listed
- The `@Man` annotation provides more detailed text about the command when we type `man activemq`
- The `@Command` annotation signals CRaSH to invoke the `ping` method when we type `activemq ping`

CRaSH provides an `InvocationContext` variable if we want it. This gives us access to information about the current session. Spring Boot Actuator embeds some extra properties inside this context shown as follows:

- `spring.boot.version`
- `spring.version`
- `spring.beanfactory`
- `spring.environment`

In this code, we use it to extract `BeanFactory` in order to grab JMS `ConnectionFactory`. Using this, we try to create a connection. If successful, the code returns `UP!`. If not, it returns `DOWN!`.

> Don't overlook that `spring.beanfactory` is all lowercase. If you try to fetch `spring.beanFactory`, it won't fail fast as a non-existent key; instead it will fetch a `null` value and probably fail later on with a null pointer exception.

After walking through the preceding `ping` command, understanding the following `metrics` command will probably be easier:

```
...
@Usage("Print out ActiveMQ metrics")
@Man("Iterate over all metrics, and print out any that
involves 'messages'")
@Command
void metrics(InvocationContext context) {
    BeanFactory beanFactory =
    context.attributes['spring.beanfactory']
    def metricRepository =
    beanFactory.getBean(MetricRepository)
    metricRepository.findAll().each { metric ->
        if (metric.name.startsWith("counter.messages")) {
            out.println "${metric.name}: ${metric.value}"
        }
    }
}

}
```

The `metrics` command has the same CRaSH machinery (`@Usage`, `@Man`, and `@Command`) as ping. However, notice that it has a return type of `void`. That's because it doesn't return anything. Instead, it prints out its results.

Inside the method, it fetches a copy of `BeanFactory`. With this, it gets ahold of the `MetricRepository` bean. This is the bean where the `CounterService` code, earlier in this chapter, stores its metrics. Our `metrics` command then iterates over all metrics, looking for ones that start with `counter.messages`. It finally prints each metric's name and value to the console.

out is provided by CRaSH when it transforms the script into a set of commands.

Having walked through all the code, let's try it out! We can launch our app and check out CRaSH, but by default it will generate a random password every time (and print that password on the console). To override it with a fixed password, we just need to supply it with `shell.auth.simple.user.password`.

In this case, let's do this on the command line using Spring Boot's alternative property setting mechanism:

```
$ SHELL_AUTH_SIMPLE_USER_PASSWORD=password ./gradlew bootRun
...

  .   ____          _            __ _ _
 /\\ / ___'_ __ _ _(_)_ __  __ _ \ \ \ \
( ( )\___ | '_ | '_| | '_ \/ _` | \ \ \ \
 \\/  ___)| |_)| | | | | || (_| |  ) ) ) )
  '  |____| .__|_| |_|_| |_\__, | / / / /
 =========|_|==============|___/=/_/_/_/
 :: Spring Boot ::        (v1.1.6.RELEASE)


2014-07-13 15:32:28.658 ... : Configuring property mail.debug=false from
prope...
2014-07-13 15:32:28.659 ... : Configuring property ssh.port=2000 from
properties
2014-07-13 15:32:28.659 ... : Configuring property auth=simple from
properties
2014-07-13 15:32:28.660 ... : Configuring property auth.simple.
username=user f...
2014-07-13 15:32:28.660 ... : Configuring property auth.simple.
password=passwo...
2014-07-13 15:32:28.667 ... : Booting SSHD
2014-07-13 15:32:28.688 ... : BouncyCastle already registered as a JCE
provider
2014-07-13 15:32:29.122 ... : About to start CRaSSHD
2014-07-13 15:32:29.142 ... : CRaSSHD started on port 2000
```

The console output has been trimmed down to CRaSH-specific things. We get the following information from the output:

- Username is `user`: This can be overridden with `shell.auth.simple.user`
- Password is `password` (though cut off due to the format of this book)
- SSH port is `2000`: This can be overridden with `shell.ssh.port`

While this is running, we can connect to another shell through SSH:

```
$ ssh -p 2000 user@localhost
Password authentication
Password:

  .   ____          _            __ _ _
 /\\ / ___'_ __ _ _(_)_ __  __ _ \ \ \ \
( ( )\___ | '_ | '_| | '_ \/ _` | \ \ \ \
 \\/  ___)| |_)| | | | | || (_| |  ) ) ) )
  '  |____| .__|_| |_|_| |_\__, | / / / /
 =========|_|==============|___/=/_/_/_/
 :: Spring Boot ::   (v1.1.6.RELEASE) on retina
```

From here, we can quickly get a listing of all the commands by typing `help`:

```
> help
Try one of these commands with the -h or --help switch:
```

NAME	DESCRIPTION
activemq	Various commands to interact with ActiveMQ JMS broker
autoconfig	Display auto configuration report from ApplicationContext
beans	Display beans in ApplicationContext
cron	manages the cron plugin
dashboard	a monitoring dashboard
egrep	search file(s) for lines that match a pattern
endpoint	Invoke actuator endpoints
env	display the term env
filter	a filter for a stream of map
java	various java language commands
jmx	Java Management Extensions
jul	java.util.logging commands
jvm	JVM informations
less	opposite of more
mail	interact with emails
man	format and display the on-line manual pages
metrics	Display metrics provided by Spring Boot
shell	shell related command

```
sleep       sleep for some time

sort        sort a map

system      vm system properties commands

thread      JVM thread commands

help        provides basic help

repl        list the repl or change the current repl
```

At the top of the commands, we see `activemq` and its top level description. Let's dig in the details of `activemq`:

```
> activemq
usage: activemq [-h | --help] COMMAND [ARGS]


The most commonly used activemq commands are:
  metrics             Print out ActiveMQ metrics
  ping                Check ActiveMQ status
```

We can see the listing of both the commands we created. This is where it displays each command's `@Usage` text.

For more details, try `man activemq`:

```
> man activemq
NAME
      activemq - Various commands to interact with ActiveMQ JMS broker


SYNOPSIS
      activemq [-h | --help] COMMAND [ARGS]


PARAMETERS
      [-h | --help]
          Display this help message


COMMANDS
      metrics
          Iterate over all metrics, and print out any that involves
'messages'


      ping
          Creates a connection to the broker. If successful, report 'UP'.
If not, report 'DOWN'
```

This shows the more detailed @Man text. Even though our code contains a single line, this is the perfect place to embed highly detailed information for the users.

Time to invoke things! First, let's check the status of our JMS broker:

```
> activemq ping
Broker is UP!
```

 Since we are using an embedded broker, it's impossible to shut down the broker and try out this command without shutting down the app. It's left as an exercise to reconfigure this application to use a standalone broker, start up this app, and then check the status of the broker with this command.

Now, let's get a read-out on our message-based metrics:

```
> activemq metrics
counter.messages.multiplex205.consumed: 25
counter.messages.multiplex205.produced: 25
counter.messages.router101.consumed: 23
counter.messages.router101.produced: 23
counter.messages.switch1143.consumed: 12
counter.messages.switch1143.produced: 12
counter.messages.total.consumed: 60
counter.messages.total.produced: 60
```

We're not going to delve into the particulars of these metrics because we have already talked about them earlier in this chapter. Instead, let's focus on how easy it was to expose already collected metrics defined earlier in this chapter. The same metrics are visible through either HTTP endpoints, JMX endpoints, or inside CRaSH (endpoint invoke metricsEndpoint).

We just have a nicer format inside CRaSH. We also took two different bits of information (health and metrics) involving ActiveMQ and served them up from a common location (the activemq commands).

This opens the door to what can be embedded as support commands inside CRaSH. We have access to the application context and can gather whatever information we need from various parts of the application.

 For more ideas and inspiration on creating management tools, watch my webinar video at http://bit.ly/app-mgmt-tools-with-boot.

Summary

In this chapter, we created a JMS-based publisher/subscribe app using embedded ActiveMQ. We used it as the means to experiment with various tools, such as Spring Boot's auto-configuration report. Using this report, we deduced what was configured (embedded versus standalone broker). We were able to reconfigure things to use a standalone broker and override Spring Boot's opinion.

We added Spring Boot's Actuator module and looked a little deeper at configuring customized health checks, application information, and metrics. We learned how to ping ActiveMQ's broker, display various application information including Git and project metadata and also gather customized metrics on message flow. We then started adjusting the settings of management endpoints, such as port, path, and URL. Then we shut off the HTTP endpoints and accessed things through JMX. Finally, we added the remote CRaSH shell, and added some custom commands.

In the next chapter, we will dive into managing application data using Spring Boot's super cool features.

4
Data Access with Spring Boot

"@springboot with @springframework is pure productivity! Who said in #java one has to write double the code than in other langs? #newFavLib"

— Frank Neff `@frank_neff`

In the previous chapter, we got our arms around the means to debug and manage apps. With all these tools, it's time to build a real app. Few applications exist that don't touch a database. In fact, data storage is arguably one of the most critical components we encounter with app development. In this chapter, we'll create an app that is used to manage sports teams and teammates. We'll persist the data to JPA and MongoDB datastores for both development and production needs.

In this chapter, we will be:

- Creating an app that writes data to an H2 in-memory dev database using Spring Boot's JPA support
- Creating entities and repositories required to manage teammate info
- Learning how to load development data using SQL scripts
- Seeing how to alternatively load data using Spring Data APIs
- Showing how to configure the app with a production profile that won't wipe and reload the data every time it starts
- Reconfiguring the application to use MongoDB instead
- Adding a profile to wipe and reload data when in development but maintain existing data when in production

Creating an app using H2's in-memory database

To create an application, we need a quick way to get off the ground. H2 (http://h2database.com) provides a very convenient in-memory database that supports JPA. It makes it really simple for development work. Using http://start.spring.io as we did in *Chapter 2, Quick Start with Java*, we can quickly create the following application build file:

```
buildscript {
    repositories {
        mavenCentral()
    }
    dependencies {
        classpath("org.springframework.boot:spring-boot-gradle-
        plugin:1.1.6.RELEASE")
    }
}

apply plugin: 'java'
apply plugin: 'spring-boot'

jar {
    baseName = 'teams'
    version =  '0.0.1-SNAPSHOT'
}
sourceCompatibility = 1.8
targetCompatibility = 1.8

repositories {
    mavenCentral()
}


dependencies {
    compile("org.springframework.boot:spring-boot-starter-
    data-jpa")
    compile("com.h2database:h2")
}

task wrapper(type: Wrapper) {
    gradleVersion = '2.1'
}
```

What do we have? Let's break down this build file:

- It pulls in `spring-boot-starter-data-jpa`, which is the Spring Boot starter that provides access to Spring Data JPA (`http://projects.spring.io/spring-data-jpa`).

- To get going, it has `com.h2database`, which is the in-memory database we were talking about earlier.

- Note that no versions are specified outside of `spring-boot-gradle-plugin`. This plugin uses Spring Boot's dependency settings to populate the version numbers for us.

Defining entities and repositories

When developing a data-oriented app, it's important to model the domain objects. For this application, we will manage `Team` and `Teammate`. The relationship between these two domain classes is defined as follows:

- A `Team` can have zero or more `Teammates`
- A `Teammate` is associated with zero or one `Teams`

Here is the definition for the `Team` class:

```
package learningspringboot;

import javax.persistence.Entity;
import javax.persistence.GeneratedValue;
import javax.persistence.Id;
import javax.persistence.OneToMany;
import java.util.ArrayList;
import java.util.List;

@Entity
public class Team {

    @Id @GeneratedValue
    private Long id;

    private String name;

    @OneToMany(mappedBy = "team")
    private List<Teammate> members;

    private Team() {
```

```
        members = new ArrayList<>();
    }

    public Team(String name) {
        this();
        this.name = name;
    }

    public String getName() {
        return name;
    }

    public void setName(String name) {
        this.name = name;
    }

    public List<Teammate> getMembers() {
        return members;
    }

    public void setMembers(List<Teammate> members) {
        this.members = members;
    }
}
```

In the preceding code, we can see the model for a team:

- The `id` attribute is managed internally. The `@Id` and `@GeneratedValue` annotations ensure that unique keys will be picked without us having to lift a finger.

- It has a name.

- It contains a list of members. The `@OneToMany` annotation indicates that this relationship is "owned" by the `Teammate` entity's table through its `team` attribute.

- We have two constructors. The `private`, no argument one is needed by JPA, but we hide it from public consumption. Instead, we have a `public` one that requires the user to supply the team's name. This ensures that no `Team` instance is created without its name.

Now let's look at the definition of the `Teammate` class:

```
package learningspringboot;

import javax.persistence.Entity;
import javax.persistence.GeneratedValue;
import javax.persistence.Id;
import javax.persistence.ManyToOne;

@Entity
public class Teammate {

    @Id @GeneratedValue
    private Long id;

    private String firstName;
    private String lastName;
    private String position;

    @ManyToOne
    private Team team;

    private Teammate() {
    }

    public Teammate(String firstName, String lastName) {
        this();
        this.firstName = firstName;
        this.lastName = lastName;
    }

    public String getFirstName() {
        return firstName;
    }

    public void setFirstName(String firstName) {
        this.firstName = firstName;
    }

    public String getLastName() {
        return lastName;
    }
```

```java
    public void setLastName(String lastName) {
        this.lastName = lastName;
    }

    public String getPosition() {
        return position;
    }

    public void setPosition(String position) {
        this.position = position;
    }

    public Team getTeam() {
        return team;
    }

    public void setTeam(Team team) {
        this.team = team;
    }

    @Override
    public String toString() {
        return id + ": " + firstName + " " + lastName + " is
        playing " + position + " for the " + team.getName();
    }
}
```

Each `Teammate` instance contains several attributes:

- The `id` attribute is managed internally.

- The `firstName`, `lastName`, and `position` attributes are simple attributes that describe a teammate.

- The `team` attribute shows us the related `Team` instance, which is linked by the `@ManyToOne` annotation.

- The constructors for `Teammate` use the same tactic as `Team`. We only expose the one that requires `firstName` and `lastName` to ensure that required fields are provided while the other one is hidden as `private`. (If JPA didn't need the empty constructor, we would remove it entirely.)

To get off the ground with Spring Data, we need to create corresponding repository interfaces based on the domain objects we just defined. First, we'll declare the `TeamRepository` interface:

```
package learningspringboot;

import org.springframework.data.repository.CrudRepository;

public interface TeamRepository extends CrudRepository<Team, Long>
{}
```

This empty interface extends Spring Data's `CrudRepository` interface, declaring it to manage `Team` entities with an ID type of `Long`.

What methods does `CrudRepository` come with? They are listed in the following table:

Method	Description
`count()`	Returns the number of entities available
`delete(ID id)`	Deletes the entity with the given `id`
`delete(Iterable<? extends T> entities)`	Deletes the given entities
`delete(T entity)`	Deletes a given entity
`deleteAll()`	Deletes all entities managed by the repository
`exists(ID id)`	Returns whether an entity with the given `id` exists
`findAll()`	Returns all instances of the type with the given IDs
`findOne(ID id)`	Retrieves an entity by its `id`
`save(Iterable<S> entites)`	Saves all given entities
`save(S entity)`	Saves a given entity

The methods shown in this table list enough operations to do all CRUD operations.

> There is also a `JpaRepository` interface that subclasses `CrudRepository`. So why aren't we using it? Because it ties us to its JPA-specific features, increasing coupling. In general, it's best to remove this dependency. This way, the only JPA requirements are the annotations that are applied to the domain objects.

Now, let's look at the definition for `TeammateRepository`:

```
package learningspringboot;

import org.springframework.data.repository.CrudRepository;

public interface TeammateRepository extends
CrudRepository<Teammate, Long> {}
```

This interface does the same, only it manages `Teammate` entities with the same ID type of `Long`.

So how do these repositories work? There is no code here or in Spring Data's repository interfaces. Search this book and you won't find any concrete details either. It's simple. Spring Data actually writes the database operations for us by creating a concrete proxy that implements the interface. The proxy manages connections and writes queries and data manipulation ops for the underlying datastore. For more details, I suggest that you read *Spring Data* by Mark Pollack, Oliver Gierke, Thomas Risberg, Jon Brisbin, and Michael Hunger. Although it was released in 2012, it provides a keen insight into the fundamentals of the various Spring Data projects.

Spring Data scans for interfaces that extend `CrudRepository`, and then it automatically creates the necessary JPA configuration. Spring Boot continues this by adding additional beans required by Spring Data, such as automatically creating the necessary `DataSource` beans along with many others.

Finally, to launch our app, we need this bit of Spring Boot glue code:

```
package learningspringboot;

import javax.annotation.PostConstruct;

import org.slf4j.Logger;
import org.slf4j.LoggerFactory;
import org.springframework.beans.factory.annotation.Autowired;
import org.springframework.boot.SpringApplication;
import org.springframework.boot.autoconfigure.EnableAutoConfiguration;
import org.springframework.context.annotation.ComponentScan;
import org.springframework.context.annotation.Configuration;

@Configuration
@ComponentScan
```

```
@EnableAutoConfiguration
public class Application {

    private static final Logger log =
    LoggerFactory.getLogger(Application.class);

    public static void main(String[] args) {
        SpringApplication.run(Application.class, args);
    }

    @Autowired
    TeammateRepository teammateRepository;

    @PostConstruct
    void seeTheRoster() {
        for (Teammate teammate : teammateRepository.findAll()) {
            log.info(teammate.toString());
        }
    }
}
```

The preceding code should look familiar:

- @Configuration: This indicates that this is a source of beans that need to be added to the application context

- @ComponentScan: This asks Spring to scan the existing package for other components, services, and configurations

- @EnableAutoConfiguration: This turns on Spring Boot's auto-configuration logic

- @Autowired TeammateRepository teammateRepository: This provides the Application class with a copy of TeammateRepository after it is created

There is a method called seeTheRoster marked with the @PostConstruct annotation. What does this method do? After all Spring beans are initialized in the application context, any methods with @PostConstruct are invoked automatically. This method is designed to use the autowired TeammateRepository instance to fetch all the teammates and print them out to console after things are properly launched. Perhaps you have noticed: we haven't loaded any data yet! Don't worry. This is covered in the next section.

While useful for demonstrations and development purposes, a method that dumps out all the database's content is not recommended for production systems.

Spring Boot's auto-configuration will detect Spring Data JPA and activate scanning for both entity types and repository interfaces.

Loading data using a SQL script

This isn't a primer on JPA. This chapter will use bits of Spring Data and JPA to show you how Spring Boot makes things simpler when accessing data. However, you should do extra reading if you aren't already familiar with JPA and the various tradeoffs you have to make for your development needs.

To get things going, we need to indicate what type of database we are using. Create `src/main/resources/application.properties` with the following settings:

```
spring.datasource.platform: h2
```

This immediately signals Spring Boot that we are using H2. Spring Boot will look for `data.sql` as well as `data-${platform}.sql` files to run. It uses Spring JDBC to do this (which was pulled in transitively by `spring-boot-starter-data-jpa`).

Having specified platform `h2`, now create `src/main/resources/data-h2.sql`, as follows:

```
insert into team
(id, name)
values
(1, 'Spring Boot Badgers');

insert into teammate
(id, first_name, last_name, position, team_id) values
(1, 'Greg', 'Turnquist', '2nd base', 1);

insert into teammate (id, first_name, last_name, position,
team_id) values
(2, 'Roy', 'Clarkson', '1st base', 1);

insert into teammate
(id, first_name, last_name, position, team_id) values
(3, 'Phil', 'Webb', 'pitcher', 1);
```

This SQL script first creates a row in the `team` table for `Spring Boot Badgers`. Then it adds rows for Greg Turnquist, Roy Clarkson, and Phil Webb to the `teammate` table—all three are linked by foreign key to that team.

It's important to note that the previous SQL code doesn't actually create the schema. Instead, Spring Boot automatically configures JPA to run in the `create-drop` mode when it detects H2. The `create-drop` mode will automatically create a schema based on the defined entities and their JPA annotations.

> Should I use what JPA provides, or configure the database schema myself? The answer comes down to what best fits your development team. Some teams develop the database schema outside of their apps. If that is your case, JPA's annotations make it super easy to line up your entities with the tables and columns. If you want Spring Boot to perform custom schema creation operations instead, create `scheme.sql` and/or `schema-${platform}.sql`. To switch off ALL database initialization, add `spring.datasource.initialize=false` to `application.properties`.

As a last step, let's log some messages from Hibernate. To do this, we need to create `src/main/resources/logback.xml`:

```xml
<?xml version="1.0" encoding="UTF-8"?>
<configuration>
    <include
    resource="org/springframework/boot/logging/logback/base.xml"/>
    <logger name="org.hibernate.SQL" level="DEBUG"/>
</configuration>
```

Let's break down the details of this logging configuration file:

- It bases itself off Spring Boot's `base.xml` logback configuration
- We add the DEBUG level logging for `org.hibernate.SQL`

What is the benefit of this setup? By simply inheriting Spring Boot's logback configuration, we don't have to think about loggers, formats, appending, and so on. Instead, we can shift immediately to log levels for specific packages, which is often all we need when customizing logging.

What is logback? Logback (http://logback.qos.ch) is meant as a successor to log4j. Spring Boot itself has no external dependencies for a particular logging system. Instead, it performs auto-configuration based on what is on the classpath. This helps with the fact that third-party libraries use different tools such as logback, slf4j, and others. We are able to configure the log levels for all these systems through a logback.xml file.

With everything configured, let's fire things up and see what happens:

```
$ ./gradlew bootRun

...

  .   ____          _            __ _ _
 /\\ / ___'_ __ _ _(_)_ __  __ _ \ \ \ \
( ( )\___ | '_ | '_| | '_ \/ _` | \ \ \ \
 \\/  ___)| |_)| | | | | || (_| |  ) ) ) )
  '  |____| .__|_| |_|_| |_\__, | / / / /
 =========|_|==============|___/=/_/_/_/
 :: Spring Boot ::        (v1.1.6.RELEASE)


2014-07-22 11:46:14.274 ... : Starting Application on retina with PID
3268 (/U...
2014-07-22 11:46:14.305 ... : Refreshing org.springframework.context.
annotatio...
2014-07-22 11:46:15.214 ... : Building JPA container EntityManagerFactory
for ...
2014-07-22 11:46:15.232 ... : HHH000204: Processing PersistenceUnitInfo [
    name: default
    ...]
2014-07-22 11:46:15.288 ... : HHH000412: Hibernate Core {4.3.5.Final}
2014-07-22 11:46:15.289 ... : HHH000206: hibernate.properties not found
2014-07-22 11:46:15.290 ... : javassist
2014-07-22 11:46:15.446 ... : HCANN000001: Hibernate Commons Annotations
{4.0....
2014-07-22 11:46:15.560 ... : HHH000400: Using dialect: org.hibernate.
dialect....
2014-07-22 11:46:15.695 ... : HHH000397: Using ASTQueryTranslatorFactory
2014-07-22 11:46:15.973 ... : HHH000227: Running hbm2ddl schema export
```

```
2014-07-22 11:46:15.974 ... : alter table teammate drop constraint FK_
qy82oywo...

2014-07-22 11:46:15.975 ... : HHH000389: Unsuccessful: alter table
teammate dr...

2014-07-22 11:46:15.975 ... : Table "TEAMMATE" not found; SQL statement:
alter table teammate drop constraint FK_qy82oywoge1gps3y762x0uix7 if
exists [4...

2014-07-22 11:46:15.975 ... : drop table team if exists

2014-07-22 11:46:15.976 ... : drop table teammate if exists

2014-07-22 11:46:15.976 ... : create table team (id bigint generated by
defaul...

2014-07-22 11:46:15.980 ... : create table teammate (id bigint generated
by de...

2014-07-22 11:46:15.981 ... : alter table teammate add constraint FK_
qy82oywog...

2014-07-22 11:46:15.990 ... : HHH000230: Schema export complete

2014-07-22 11:46:16.071 ... : Executing SQL script from URL [file:/Users/
gturn...

2014-07-22 11:46:16.076 ... : Executed SQL script from URL [file:/Users/
gturnq...

2014-07-22 11:46:16.341 ... : select teammate0_.id as id1_1_, teammate0_.
first...

2014-07-22 11:46:16.353 ... : select team0_.id as id1_0_0_, team0_.name
as nam...

2014-07-22 11:46:16.367 ... : 1: Greg Turnquist is playing 2nd base for
the Sp...

2014-07-22 11:46:16.367 ... : 2: Roy Clarkson is playing 1st base for the
Spri...

2014-07-22 11:46:16.368 ... : 3: Phil Webb is playing pitcher for the
Spring B...

2014-07-22 11:46:16.555 ... : Registering beans for JMX exposure on
startup

2014-07-22 11:46:16.573 ... : Started Application in 2.521 seconds (JVM
runnin...

2014-07-22 11:46:16.574 ... : Closing org.springframework.context.
annotation.A...

2014-07-22 11:46:16.575 ... : Unregistering JMX-exposed beans on shutdown

2014-07-22 11:46:16.577 ... : Closing JPA EntityManagerFactory for
persistence...

2014-07-22 11:46:16.578 ... : HHH000227: Running hbm2ddl schema export
```

```
2014-07-22 11:46:16.579 ... : alter table teammate drop constraint FK_
qy82oywo...
2014-07-22 11:46:16.580 ... : drop table team if exists
2014-07-22 11:46:16.581 ... : drop table teammate if exists
2014-07-22 11:46:16.582 ... : HHH000230: Schema export complete
```

What does the preceding console output show? Take a look at the following bullets:

- `Building JPA container`: We definitely have a JPA-based system running
- `create table team` and `create table teammate`: These statements show that Spring Boot is creating the database schema on our behalf
- `Executing SQL script from URL`: Spring Boot is running our `data-h2.sql` script as desired
- `select teammate0_.id...` and `select team0_.id...`: This is the JPA query that fetches the team roster
- `1: Greg Turnquist is playing 2nd base...`: This and the other two teammates are being printed, verifying that they were successfully loaded earlier

 As shown earlier in this book, we are using `gradlew`, which is the Gradle wrapper; it saves users of your project from having to install Gradle themselves. To create a wrapper, you need to have Gradle installed and then run `gradle wrapper`. It will create the files required for you to run the commands throughout this chapter.

Loading data programmatically

What if we don't care for SQL? Or, what if we prefer to write code and let the compiler point out flaws in our setup? The alternative is to create a database-loading class using Spring Data APIs to do the heavy lifting:

```java
package learningspringboot;

import javax.annotation.PostConstruct;

import org.springframework.beans.factory.annotation.Autowired;
import org.springframework.stereotype.Service;

@Service
```

```
public class DatabaseLoader {

    private final TeammateRepository teammateRepository;
    private final TeamRepository teamRepository;

    @Autowired
    public DatabaseLoader(TeammateRepository teammateRepository,
                          TeamRepository teamRepository) {
        this.teammateRepository = teammateRepository;
        this.teamRepository = teamRepository;
    }

    @PostConstruct
    private void initDatabase() {
        Team springBootTeam = new Team("Spring Boot Badgers");
        teamRepository.save(springBootTeam);

        Teammate greg = new Teammate("Greg", "Turnquist");
        greg.setPosition("2nd base");
        greg.setTeam(springBootTeam);
        teammateRepository.save(greg);

        Teammate roy = new Teammate("Roy", "Clarkson");
        roy.setPosition("1st base");
        roy.setTeam(springBootTeam);
        teammateRepository.save(roy);

        Teammate phil = new Teammate("Phil", "Webb");
        phil.setPosition("pitcher");
        phil.setTeam(springBootTeam);
        teammateRepository.save(phil);
    }

}
```

This is how we can programmatically create entries in the database. To see how it works, let's break it down:

- `@Service`: This indicates that this class should be picked up during Spring's component scanning

- `@Autowired`: Spring will automatically supply `teammateRepository` and `teamRepository` to the constructor when creating this bean

- `@PostConstruct`: After the bean is created, Spring will run `initDatabase`, initializing the database

Let's look a little closer at how one specific player gets loaded inside `initDatabase`:

```
Teammate roy = new Teammate("Roy", "Clarkson");
roy.setPosition("1st base");
roy.setTeam(springBootTeam);
```

In this fragment, we can see:

- A new `Teammate` object is created. The constructor requires that we provide first and last names.
- We configure the player's position.
- We identify what team the player is associated with (an optional setting).
- We save the new teammate using the autowired `teammateRepository` instance.
- We do not set the `id`. (It's handled automatically.)

Earlier in this chapter, we discussed how Spring Data essentially writes the database operations for us when we define repository interfaces. For the simplest operations, we don't have to lift a finger.

Spring Data makes it easy to create finder methods. If we add `List<Teammate> findByPosition(String position)` to `TeammateRepository`, Spring Data will automatically craft a query to retrieve all teammates that have the designated position. For queries that are more complex than properties, we can apply `@Query("custom query")` to a given method and write our own query using **SpEL (Spring Expression Language)**. As this chapter is about getting up and running and not delving into Spring Data itself, we won't create any query.

Next, we must delete `data-h2.sql` and remove `application.properties`.

We also have to make some slight alterations to the main `Application` class:

```
package learningspringboot;

import javax.annotation.PostConstruct;

import org.slf4j.Logger;
import org.slf4j.LoggerFactory;
import org.springframework.beans.factory.annotation.Autowired;
import org.springframework.boot.SpringApplication;
```

```
import org.springframework.boot.autoconfigure.EnableAutoConfiguration;
import org.springframework.context.annotation.ComponentScan;
import org.springframework.context.annotation.Configuration;

@Configuration
@ComponentScan
@EnableAutoConfiguration
public class Application {

    private static final Logger log =
    LoggerFactory.getLogger(Application.class);

    public static void main(String[] args) {
        SpringApplication.run(Application.class, args);
    }

    @Autowired
    DatabaseLoader databaseLoader;

    @Autowired
    TeammateRepository teammateRepository;

    @PostConstruct
    void seeTheRoster() {
        for (Teammate teammate : teammateRepository.findAll()) {
            log.info(teammate.toString());
        }
    }
}
```

What changed from the previous version of `Application`? Just one thing: we added `DatabaseLoader` as an autowired dependency inside the `Application` class.

What does that mean? We don't actually use it anywhere, but it ensures that `DatabaseLoader` is created before `Application` from a dependency injection point of view. The side effect is that the `DatabaseLoader` class' `initDatabase` method will run before the `Application` class' `seeTheRoster` method.

> As an alternative to asking for an autowired copy of `DatabaseLoader`, we could have put `@DependsOn("databaseLoader")` as a class-level annotation on `Application`. It would have also ensured that `initDatabase` was run before `seeTheRoster`. However, later on in this chapter, we will alter this autowiring to detect whether or not the development data has been loaded, so we are keeping things as they are.

The output will look like this:

```
     .   ____          _            __ _ _
    /\\ / ___'_ __ _ _(_)_ __  __ _ \ \ \ \
   ( ( )\___ | '_ | '_| | '_ \/ _' | \ \ \ \
    \\/  ___)| |_)| | | | | || (_| |  ) ) ) )
     '  |____| .__|_| |_|_| |_\__, | / / / /
    =========|_|==============|___/=/_/_/_/
    :: Spring Boot ::        (v1.1.6.RELEASE)


2014-07-24 21:57:55.533 ... : Starting Application on retina with PID
3727 (/U...
2014-07-24 21:57:55.560 ... : Refreshing org.springframework.context.
annotatio...
2014-07-24 21:57:56.454 ... : Building JPA container EntityManagerFactory
for ...
2014-07-24 21:57:56.473 ... : HHH000204: Processing PersistenceUnitInfo [
   name: default
   ...]
2014-07-24 21:57:56.528 ... : HHH000412: Hibernate Core {4.3.5.Final}
2014-07-24 21:57:56.530 ... : HHH000206: hibernate.properties not found
2014-07-24 21:57:56.531 ... : javassist
2014-07-24 21:57:56.684 ... : HCANN000001: Hibernate Commons Annotations
{4.0....
2014-07-24 21:57:56.785 ... : HHH000400: Using dialect: org.hibernate.
dialect....
2014-07-24 21:57:56.917 ... : HHH000397: Using ASTQueryTranslatorFactory
2014-07-24 21:57:57.191 ... : HHH000227: Running hbm2ddl schema export
2014-07-24 21:57:57.192 ... : alter table teammate drop constraint FK_
qy82oywo...
2014-07-24 21:57:57.193 ... : HHH000389: Unsuccessful: alter table
teammate dr...
2014-07-24 21:57:57.193 ... : Table "TEAMMATE" not found; SQL statement:
alter table teammate drop constraint FK_qy82oywogelgps3y762x0uix7 if
exists [4...
2014-07-24 21:57:57.193 ... : drop table team if exists
2014-07-24 21:57:57.193 ... : drop table teammate if exists
```

```
2014-07-24 21:57:57.194 ... : create table team (id bigint generated by
defaul...
2014-07-24 21:57:57.197 ... : create table teammate (id bigint generated
by de...
2014-07-24 21:57:57.199 ... : alter table teammate add constraint FK_
qy82oywog...
2014-07-24 21:57:57.205 ... : HHH000230: Schema export complete
2014-07-24 21:57:57.454 ... : insert into team (id, name) values (null,
?)
2014-07-24 21:57:57.471 ... : insert into teammate (id, first_name, last_
name,...
2014-07-24 21:57:57.473 ... : insert into teammate (id, first_name, last_
name,...
2014-07-24 21:57:57.474 ... : insert into teammate (id, first_name, last_
name,...
2014-07-24 21:57:57.578 ... : select teammate0_.id as id1_1_, teammate0_.
first...
2014-07-24 21:57:57.586 ... : select team0_.id as id1_0_0_, team0_.name
as nam...
2014-07-24 21:57:57.593 ... : 1: Greg Turnquist is playing 2nd base for
the Sp...
2014-07-24 21:57:57.593 ... : 2: Roy Clarkson is playing 1st base for the
Spri...
2014-07-24 21:57:57.593 ... : 3: Phil Webb is playing pitcher for the
Spring B...
2014-07-24 21:57:57.762 ... : Registering beans for JMX exposure on
startup
2014-07-24 21:57:57.782 ... : Started Application in 2.435 seconds (JVM
runnin...
2014-07-24 21:57:57.784 ... : Closing org.springframework.context.
annotation.A...
2014-07-24 21:57:57.785 ... : Unregistering JMX-exposed beans on shutdown
2014-07-24 21:57:57.787 ... : Closing JPA EntityManagerFactory for
persistence...
2014-07-24 21:57:57.788 ... : HHH000227: Running hbm2ddl schema export
2014-07-24 21:57:57.789 ... : alter table teammate drop constraint FK_
qy82oywo...
2014-07-24 21:57:57.790 ... : drop table team if exists
2014-07-24 21:57:57.792 ... : drop table teammate if exists
2014-07-24 21:57:57.793 ... : HHH000230: Schema export complete
```

This looks very similar to the previous output. The key differences are that instead of seeing `Executing SQL script`, we see `insert into team` and `insert into teammate`.

With these two scenarios (the **Loading data using a SQL script** section versus the *Loading data programmatically* section), the choice you make comes down to taste. Programmatically loading data takes up more space, but it ensures that things are being created in compliance with the defined APIs. SQL is much more explicit about what is happening, but it requires that we manage all the primary and foreign keys correctly. SQL is also more compact.

 Am I forced to make a global decision about using SQL or Spring Data to insert data? Not really. For general development, you can write a SQL script. However, for specific unit tests, you might insert data using Spring Data repositories. Or you might wish to do things the other way around. It comes down to what you and your team prefer.

Adding a production profile for a MySQL database

So far, we've built a pretty simple system. It bootstraps an in-memory database, preloads a team with three players, and then gives us a printout of the roster on the console. So, what happens when it's time to deploy this into production? There are several issues with using an in-memory database when it comes to production, and these issues are listed as follows:

- An in-memory database isn't persistent across restarts.
- By default, Spring Boot configures H2 to `create-drop` the database. This means that the database is wiped and reloaded every time.
- The production database server most certainly is not running on our desktop. We have to tell Spring Boot where to connect and how.
- It's possible that we the developers won't even be granted access to the database credentials. How do we handle that?

We could scrap all the settings used up to this point, but that would destroy valuable work. It would also hinder our ability to continue working on the app in the development mode. The solution is to use Spring's environmental profiles.

For starters, assuming our production database is MySQL, let's add MySQL's JDBC library to our list of dependencies in `build.gradle`:

```
compile("mysql:mysql-connector-java")
```

 The `mysql-connector-java` package is another third-party dependency where the version number is supplied by Spring Boot.

If we ran `Application.main` right now, nothing would change. Spring Boot is hardwired so that if it spots H2 (or HSQL or Derby) it will run things in an embedded, development mode. Spring Boot will automatically create connectors for the in-memory database and also set it to the `create-drop` mode. This is good, because it will let us continue working in the development mode until we make some clear changes.

The next step toward a production configuration is to create `src/main/resources/application-production.properties`, which is shown as follows:

```
spring.jpa.hibernate.ddl-auto=none

spring.datasource.url=jdbc:mysql://localhost/your-db-name
spring.datasource.username=your-user-name
spring.datasource.password=your-password
spring.datasource.driverClassName=com.mysql.jdbc.Driver
```

 You must plug in your own connection URL and username/password.

There are several things happening here:

- We named it `application-production.properties` to indicate that this property file is only loaded by Spring Boot when `spring.profiles.active` contains `production`
- The `spring.jpa.hibernate.ddl-auto` property is set to `none`, which means that it will do nothing about creating the schema or dropping tables when the app finishes
- The `spring.datasource` properties contain the necessary settings so that Hibernate can connect

Hibernate's `ddl-auto` options are: `none`, `validate`, `update`, and `create-drop`. create-drop is the default setting for H2, HSQL, and Derby databases. For anything else, Spring Boot defaults to none.

What are Spring profiles? Spring makes it easy to segregate the creation of beans based on custom profile settings. Individual beans or entire collections of bean definitions can be flagged to only work based on the profile that is active. Spring Boot dials this up further by supporting `application-${profile}.properties` files that are only tapped in a similar fashion. For a more in-depth tutorial, read `http://spring.io/blog/2011/02/14/spring-3-1-m1-introducing-profile` (note that the blog entry is pre-Spring Boot).

The following change must be made to `DatabaseLoader`:

```
@Service
@Profile("!production")
public class DatabaseLoader {
```

The `@Profile` annotation indicates that the `DatabaseLoader` class will only activate and begin initializing the database if Spring is not running with the `production` profile.

One other change inside `Application` is in order:

```
@Autowired(required = false)
DatabaseLoader databaseLoader;
```

We previously autowired `DatabaseLoader` to ensure that the data was loaded before trying to print out the roster. However, if we are running in the production mode, this bean wouldn't have been created. So we mark it as `(required = false)`.

With these handful of changes to our app, we can run `Application.main` again from inside our IDE. It should run fine (assuming we installed and launched a standalone MySQL database).

A key indicator that things are running in the development mode inside our IDE is when we see `Using dialect: org.hibernate.dialect.H2Dialect` in the output. This indicates that it is running H2, the embedded database. Furthermore, we should see the same roster printed out as the one we saw earlier in this chapter.

Now, if we run our app from the console and turn on the `production` profile, we should see something like this:

```
$ SPRING_PROFILES_ACTIVE=production ./gradlew bootRun

...

   .   ____          _            __ _ _
  /\\ / ___'_ __ _ _(_)_ __  __ _ \ \ \ \
 ( ( )\___ | '_ | '_| | '_ \/ _` | \ \ \ \
  \\/  ___)| |_)| | | | | || (_| |  ) ) ) )
   '  |____| .__|_| |_|_| |_\__, | / / / /
 =========|_|==============|___/=/_/_/_/
 :: Spring Boot ::        (v1.1.6.RELEASE)


2014-07-24 23:04:14.679 ... : Starting Application on retina with PID
4217 (/U...
2014-07-24 23:04:14.708 ... : Refreshing org.springframework.context.
annotatio...
2014-07-24 23:04:15.438 ... : Building JPA container EntityManagerFactory
for ...
2014-07-24 23:04:15.458 ... : HHH000204: Processing PersistenceUnitInfo [
    name: default
    ...]
2014-07-24 23:04:15.511 ... : HHH000412: Hibernate Core {4.3.5.Final}
2014-07-24 23:04:15.513 ... : HHH000206: hibernate.properties not found
2014-07-24 23:04:15.514 ... : javassist
2014-07-24 23:04:15.623 ... : HCANN000001: Hibernate Commons Annotations
{4.0....
2014-07-24 23:04:15.964 ... : HHH000400: Using dialect: org.hibernate.
dialect.MySQL5Dialect
2014-07-24 23:04:16.130 ... : HHH000397: Using ASTQueryTranslatorFactory
2014-07-24 23:04:16.754 ... : select teammate0_.id as id1_1_, teammate0_.
first...
2014-07-24 23:04:16.774 ... : SQL Error: 1146, SQLState: 42S02
2014-07-24 23:04:16.775 ... : Table 'test.teammate' doesn't exist
2014-07-24 23:04:16.780 ... : Closing JPA EntityManagerFactory for
persistence...
2014-07-24 23:04:16.783 ... : Application failed to start with classpath:
[fil...
```

First of all, we can see that the app is trying to talk to a MySQL database because of this: `Using dialect: org.hibernate.dialect.MySQL5Dialect`.

However, something went terribly wrong! According to the last message shown in the preceding output, the application had a failure on startup. Digging in, we find that `Table 'test.teammate' doesn't exist` is the first clue. Further along in the output (and not shown in the preceding output due to format restrictions), this becomes clear when we see `org.hibernate.exception.SQLGrammarException: could not extract ResultSet`. It appears that the app tried to query a table that doesn't exist.

This is what happens if you run the application in the production mode but don't initialize the database with the schema and sample data.

 This scenario is highly unlikely. Either you or your DBA will have most likely built and run some script to set up the database properly.

Instead of writing a separate script, let's simply switch `spring.jpa.hibernate.ddl-auto` to update and comment out `@Profile("!production")` from `DatabaseLoader`. Then run the app again:

```
$ SPRING_PROFILES_ACTIVE=production ./gradlew bootRun

...

  .   ____          _            __ _ _
 /\\ / ___'_ __ _ _(_)_ __  __ _ \ \ \ \
( ( )\___ | '_ | '_| | '_ \/ _` | \ \ \ \
 \\/  ___)| |_)| | | | | || (_| |  ) ) ) )
  '  |____| .__|_| |_|_| |_\__, | / / / /
 =========|_|==============|___/=/_/_/_/
 :: Spring Boot ::        (v1.1.6.RELEASE)


2014-07-24 23:35:53.930 ... : Starting Application on retina with PID
5191 (/U...
2014-07-24 23:35:53.960 ... : Refreshing org.springframework.context.
annotatio...
2014-07-24 23:35:54.709 ... : Building JPA container EntityManagerFactory
for ...
2014-07-24 23:35:54.726 ... : HHH000204: Processing PersistenceUnitInfo [
    name: default
    ...]
```

```
2014-07-24 23:35:54.781 ... : HHH000412: Hibernate Core {4.3.5.Final}

2014-07-24 23:35:54.782 ... : HHH000206: hibernate.properties not found

2014-07-24 23:35:54.783 ... : javassist

2014-07-24 23:35:54.900 ... : HCANN000001: Hibernate Commons Annotations
{4.0....

2014-07-24 23:35:55.246 ... : HHH000400: Using dialect: org.hibernate.
dialect....

2014-07-24 23:35:55.424 ... : HHH000397: Using ASTQueryTranslatorFactory

2014-07-24 23:35:55.653 ... : HHH000228: Running hbm2ddl schema update

2014-07-24 23:35:55.653 ... : HHH000102: Fetching database metadata

2014-07-24 23:35:55.654 ... : HHH000396: Updating schema

2014-07-24 23:35:55.658 ... : HHH000262: Table not found: team

2014-07-24 23:35:55.659 ... : HHH000262: Table not found: teammate

2014-07-24 23:35:55.660 ... : HHH000262: Table not found: team

2014-07-24 23:35:55.660 ... : HHH000262: Table not found: teammate

2014-07-24 23:35:55.661 ... : HHH000262: Table not found: team

2014-07-24 23:35:55.662 ... : HHH000262: Table not found: teammate

2014-07-24 23:35:55.753 ... : HHH000232: Schema update complete

2014-07-24 23:35:56.086 ... : insert into team (name) values (?)

2014-07-24 23:35:56.116 ... : insert into teammate (first_name, last_
name, pos...

2014-07-24 23:35:56.119 ... : insert into teammate (first_name, last_
name, pos...

2014-07-24 23:35:56.122 ... : insert into teammate (first_name, last_
name, pos...

2014-07-24 23:35:56.221 ... : select teammate0_.id as id1_1_, teammate0_.
first...

2014-07-24 23:35:56.226 ... : select team0_.id as id1_0_0_, team0_.name
as nam...

2014-07-24 23:35:56.235 ... : 1: Greg Turnquist is playing 2nd base for
the Sp...

2014-07-24 23:35:56.236 ... : 2: Roy Clarkson is playing 1st base for the
Spri...

2014-07-24 23:35:56.236 ... : 3: Phil Webb is playing pitcher for the
Spring B...

2014-07-24 23:35:56.355 ... : Registering beans for JMX exposure on
startup

2014-07-24 23:35:56.367 ... : Started Application in 2.62 seconds (JVM
running...
```

```
2014-07-24 23:35:56.368 ... : Closing org.springframework.context.
annotation.A...

2014-07-24 23:35:56.369 ... : Unregistering JMX-exposed beans on shutdown

2014-07-24 23:35:56.371 ... : Closing JPA EntityManagerFactory for
persistence...
```

The preceding console output shows us clear evidence of the database structure
being created as well as data being inserted:

- `Updating schema`
- `Schema update complete`
- `insert into team (name) values (?)`
- `insert into teammate...`

> This is quite handy. So why did we set things up with `ddl-auto:
> none` in the first place? Because in all likelihood, a real production
> database would have been created outside the scope of our application.
> This is in this book primarily for demonstration purposes.

To continue with this chapter's teammate app, we can switch to the preferred setting
of `ddl-auto: none` now that we have configured the table structure. To do this,
we must revert those last edits to `application-production.properties` and
`DatabaseLoader.java`. If we run things again, we should see the following in our
console output:

```
...
2014-07-24 23:40:30.454 ... : HHH000400: Using dialect: org.hibernate.
dialect....

2014-07-24 23:40:30.643 ... : HHH000397: Using ASTQueryTranslatorFactory

2014-07-24 23:40:31.177 ... : select teammate0_.id as id1_1_, teammate0_.
first...

2014-07-24 23:40:31.297 ... : select team0_.id as id1_0_0_, team0_.name
as nam...

2014-07-24 23:40:31.316 ... : 1: Greg Turnquist is playing 2nd base for
the Sp...

2014-07-24 23:40:31.316 ... : 2: Roy Clarkson is playing 1st base for the
Spri...

2014-07-24 23:40:31.316 ... : 3: Phil Webb is playing pitcher for the
Spring B...

...
```

We are now able to query a functioning, production-grade database. There are no table creation operations at the beginning and no table dropping at the end. Instead, we simply connect to the system and run our query, fetching the team roster.

 This chapter isn't going to dive into the details of migrating database schemas as you evolve your application. Instead, you can read `http://docs.spring.io/spring-boot/docs/1.1.6.RELEASE/reference/htmlsingle/#howto-use-a-higher-level-database-migration-tool` to see how Spring Boot supports both Flyway (`http://flywaydb.org`) and Liquibase (`http://www.liquibase.org`).

Adding Spring Data REST and using it to manage teammates

So far, this application has provided us with a nice API that creates and manages teammates. However, we haven't built any UI. We could start crafting a classic server-side solution by creating some templates that perform various CRUD operations. But a more modern solution would be to create a RESTful frontend that can be used to create an independent UI.

Why is is better to decouple the frontend from the backend? Let's find out:

- For starters, the frontend and backend can have different rates of change and different technology stacks, and can be supported by different pools of developer talent.

- Decoupling the frontend from the backend introduces the option to have a web frontend, an iOS frontend, and an Android frontend (and others).

- Managing three frontends and a backend with one team can generate many unintended side effects in the architecture. Decoupling forces everyone to assess changes that cross these boundaries.

- As a bonus, such decoupling opens the door to third-party companies that build clients to interact with our backend in a fashion that can be monetized.

Spring MVC has had RESTful support since Spring 3.0. We could create our RESTful API by hand, but it would be labor-intensive. Instead, we can use Spring Data REST to export our repositories automatically.

To get started, we only have to add `spring-boot-starter-data-rest` to our list of dependencies in `build.gradle`:

```
compile("org.springframework.boot:spring-boot-starter-data-rest")
```

This starter will pull in critical parts required to build RESTful services, as shown in the following table:

Module	Description
Spring Web MVC	Contains Spring REST components
Spring HATEOAS	Supplements Spring's REST support with hypermedia (http://roy.gbiv.com/untangled/2008/rest-apis-must-be-hypertext-driven)
Jackson 2	JSON serialization and deserialization library

> What is HATEOAS? Apart from being an acronym with a dozen pronunciations, it stands for **Hypermedia As The Engine Of Application State**. It was documented in Roy Fielding's PhD dissertation, which is where REST was born. Another expression for HATEOAS is hypermedia. Spring HATEOAS makes it super simple to generate hypermedia links to Spring MVC endpoints and serve them up to end users.

With this small addition to our dependencies, Spring Boot will automatically export all repository interfaces. If we launch `Application.main` in the development mode (not production mode), we can see the following console output:

```
$ ./gradlew bootRun
...
2014-08-01 22:48:13.966 ... : create table team (id bigint generated by
defaul...
2014-08-01 22:48:13.970 ... : create table teammate (id bigint generated
by de...
2014-08-01 22:48:13.971 ... : alter table teammate add constraint FK_
qy82oywog...
2014-08-01 22:48:13.978 ... : HHH000230: Schema export complete
2014-08-01 22:48:14.636 ... : Mapping servlet: 'dispatcherServlet' to [/]
2014-08-01 22:48:14.640 ... : Mapping filter: 'hiddenHttpMethodFilter'
to: [/*]
2014-08-01 22:48:14.820 ... : insert into team (id, name) values (null,
?)
```

```
2014-08-01 22:48:14.843 ... : insert into teammate (id, first_name, last_
name,...

2014-08-01 22:48:14.846 ... : insert into teammate (id, first_name, last_
name,...

2014-08-01 22:48:14.848 ... : insert into teammate (id, first_name, last_
name,...

2014-08-01 22:48:14.968 ... : select teammate0_.id as id1_1_, teammate0_.
first...

2014-08-01 22:48:14.976 ... : select team0_.id as id1_0_0_, team0_.name
as nam...

2014-08-01 22:48:14.984 ... : 1: Greg Turnquist is playing 2nd base for
the Sp...

2014-08-01 22:48:14.984 ... : 2: Roy Clarkson is playing 1st base for the
Spri...

2014-08-01 22:48:14.984 ... : 3: Phil Webb is playing pitcher for the
Spring B...

...

2014-08-01 22:48:15.404 ... : Mapped "{[/{repository}/{id}/
{property}],methods...

2014-08-01 22:48:15.404 ... : Mapped "{[/{repository}/{id}/{property}/
{propert...

2014-08-01 22:48:15.405 ... : Mapped "{[/{repository}/{id}/
{property}],methods...

2014-08-01 22:48:15.405 ... : Mapped "{[/{repository}/{id}/
{property}],methods...

2014-08-01 22:48:15.405 ... : Mapped "{[/{repository}/{id}/
{property}],methods...

2014-08-01 22:48:15.405 ... : Mapped "{[/{repository}/{id}/{property}/
{propert...

2014-08-01 22:48:15.406 ... : Mapped "{[/{repository}/
schema],methods=[GET],pa...

2014-08-01 22:48:15.409 ... : Mapped "{[/{repository}],methods=[GET],para
ms=[]...

2014-08-01 22:48:15.409 ... : Mapped "{[/{repository}],methods=[HEAD],par
ams=[...

2014-08-01 22:48:15.410 ... : Mapped "{[/{repository}],methods=[GET],para
ms=[]...

2014-08-01 22:48:15.410 ... : Mapped "{[/{repository}],methods=[POST],par
ams=[...

2014-08-01 22:48:15.410 ... : Mapped "{[/{repository}/
{id}],methods=[HEAD],par...
```

```
2014-08-01 22:48:15.410 ... : Mapped "{ [/{repository}/
{id}],methods=[GET],para...

2014-08-01 22:48:15.410 ... : Mapped "{ [/{repository}/
{id}],methods=[PUT],para...

2014-08-01 22:48:15.411 ... : Mapped "{ [/{repository}/
{id}],methods=[PATCH],pa...

2014-08-01 22:48:15.411 ... : Mapped "{ [/{repository}/
{id}],methods=[DELETE],p...

2014-08-01 22:48:15.412 ... : Mapped "{ [/],methods=[GET],params=[],
headers=[],...

2014-08-01 22:48:15.413 ... : Mapped "{ [/{repository}/
search],methods=[GET],pa...

2014-08-01 22:48:15.414 ... : Mapped "{ [/{repository}/
search],methods=[HEAD],p...

2014-08-01 22:48:15.414 ... : Mapped "{ [/{repository}/search/
{search}],methods...

2014-08-01 22:48:15.414 ... : Mapped "{ [/{repository}/search/
{search}],methods...

2014-08-01 22:48:15.414 ... : Mapped "{ [/{repository}/search/
{search}],methods...

2014-08-01 22:48:15.470 ... : Registering beans for JMX exposure on
startup

2014-08-01 22:48:15.565 ... : Tomcat started on port(s): 8080/http

2014-08-01 22:48:15.567 ... : Started Application in 5.539 seconds (JVM
runnin...
```

The preceding console output shows us the same creation of the Spring Boot Badgers and its players. However, it creates additional Spring MVC endpoints. The endpoints are heavily parameterized (/{repository}, /{repository}/{id}, /{repository}/{id}/{property}, and so on.).

Instead of decrypting all these new endpoints shown on the console, we can investigate using a REST client instead. For any *nix or Mac machine, curl on the command line is quite useful:

```
$ curl -i localhost:8080
HTTP/1.1 200 OK
Server: Apache-Coyote/1.1
Content-Type: application/hal+json
Transfer-Encoding: chunked
Date: Sat, 02 Aug 2014 03:58:02 GMT

{
```

```
"_links" : {
  "teams" : {
    "href" : "http://localhost:8080/teams"
  },
  "teammates" : {
    "href" : "http://localhost:8080/teammates"
  }
}
}
```

What is this output we are seeing? According to `Content-Type`, its media type is `application/hal+json`. This media type is found in the HAL specification (`http://tools.ietf.org/html/draft-kelly-json-hal-06`). As stated by the author of the HAL spec, *Adopting HAL will make your API explorable, and its documentation easily discoverable from within the API itself.* HAL basically includes links to other resources stored in an adjacent entry called `_links` with logical names known as **rels (relationships)**.

The preceding output has two rels, which are `teams` and `teammates`.

 For RESTful services, it's important to not get hung up on the URI of various parts of an API. These can change. Instead, we should navigate by way of relationships.

Let's look up `teams` first. The previous document tells us that to find all teams, we must navigate to its related link as follows:

```
$ curl -i localhost:8080/teams
{
  "_embedded" : {
    "teams" : [ {
      "name" : "Spring Boot Badgers",
      "_links" : {
        "self" : {
          "href" : "http://localhost:8080/teams/1"
        },
        "members" : {
          "href" : "http://localhost:8080/teams/1/members"
        }
      }
    } ]
  }
}
```

Let's walk through this preceding HAL document:

- `_embedded`: This is used for embedded resources. Spring Data REST uses it to serve up collections.
- `teams`: This is the resource we seek. It's an array with one entry for the Spring Boot Badgers.
- `name`: This is a property found inside `Team`.
- `_links`: This shows us a list of related links.
- `self`: A standard resource includes a link to itself. This is the RESTful equivalent of Java's `this` keyword.
- `members`: This is a link from `Team` that shows us members related to this team.

 For more details about Spring Data REST, check out my presentation at SpringOne 2014 at `http://www.infoq.com/presentations/spring-data-rest`. For the corresponding slide deck, see `https://speakerdeck.com/gregturn/springone2gx-2014-spring-data-rest-data-meets-hypermedia`.

So, let's look up Spring Boot Badgers with the following command:

```
$ curl localhost:8080/teams/1
{
  "name" : "Spring Boot Badgers",
  "_links" : {
    "self" : {
      "href" : "http://localhost:8080/teams/1"
    },
    "members" : {
      "href" : "http://localhost:8080/teams/1/members"
    }
  }
}
```

This appears almost identical to the previous HAL document. The only difference is that this isn't embedded data. If there were more teams, the previous HAL document would have listed them all. However, this most recent HAL document shows us only one particular team. Naturally, it has the same data.

What's more interesting is how we can use this resource's hypermedia to find the related members, as follows:

```
$ curl localhost:8080/teams/1/members
{
  "_embedded" : {
    "teammates" : [ {
      "firstName" : "Greg",
      "lastName" : "Turnquist",
      "position" : "2nd base",
      "_links" : {
        "self" : {
          "href" : "http://localhost:8080/teammates/1"
        },
        "team" : {
          "href" : "http://localhost:8080/teammates/1/team"
        }
      }
    }, {
      "firstName" : "Roy",
      "lastName" : "Clarkson",
      "position" : "1st base",
      "_links" : {
        "self" : {
          "href" : "http://localhost:8080/teammates/2"
        },
        "team" : {
          "href" : "http://localhost:8080/teammates/2/team"
        }
      }
    }, {
      "firstName" : "Phil",
      "lastName" : "Webb",
      "position" : "pitcher",
      "_links" : {
        "self" : {
```

```
          "href" : "http://localhost:8080/teammates/3"
        },
        "team" : {
          "href" : "http://localhost:8080/teammates/3/team"
        }
      }
    } ]
  }
}
```

In the preceding console output, we see our familiar teammates Greg, Roy, and Phil. Their attributes are served up along with a `self` link and a `team` link.

We can navigate every last link, but we've already seen all the data the current data model contains. It would be much more interesting to create new data. Let's kick things off by creating a new player, shown as follows:

```
$ curl -i -X POST -H 'Content-Type:application/json' -d
'{"firstName":"Dave", "lastName":"Syer", "position":"catcher"}'
localhost:8080/teammates
HTTP/1.1 201 Created
Server: Apache-Coyote/1.1
Location: http://localhost:8080/teammates/4
Content-Length: 0
Date: Sat, 02 Aug 2014 04:33:39 GMT
```

This command has several arguments, which are detailed as follows:

- `-i`: This shows us all the response headers
- `-X POST`: This switches from curl's default GET to POST to create a new resource
- `-H 'Content-Type:application/json'`: This shows that data sent over the wire to the server is JSON
- `-d '{"firstName":"Dave", "lastName":"Syer", "position":"catcher"}'`: This is the JSON representation of a new resource
- `localhost:8080/teammates`: This is the resource to use for creating new Teammate resources
- `Location: http://localhost:8080/teammates/4`: This is the response header that indicates where the newly created resource can be found

Given the `Location` header, let's look up our new resource:

```
$ curl localhost:8080/teammates/4
{
  "firstName" : "Dave",
  "lastName" : "Syer",
  "position" : "catcher",
  "_links" : {
    "self" : {
      "href" : "http://localhost:8080/teammates/4"
    },
    "team" : {
      "href" : "http://localhost:8080/teammates/4/team"
    }
  }
}
```

Everything appears to be in order. We can see the name and position that was provided through the POST request earlier.

What can we expect to find if we check on the new teammate's team? Take a look:

```
$ curl -i http://localhost:8080/teammates/4/team
HTTP/1.1 404 Not Found
Server: Apache-Coyote/1.1
Content-Length: 0
Date: Sat, 02 Aug 2014 04:43:21 GMT
```

The `404 Not Found` response code matches the fact that we haven't associated our new teammate with any team. If we want to alter the record, we have two choices: PUT or PATCH.

> PUT (`http://www.w3.org/Protocols/rfc2616/rfc2616-sec9.html#sec9.6`) is used to replace an entire resource. PATCH (`http://tools.ietf.org/html/rfc5789`) is used to update parts of a resource. For any attributes not specified with a PUT, Spring Data REST will replace them with **null**. For a PATCH, Spring Data REST ignores unspecified attributes.

Let's assign Dave to the Spring Boot Badgers with the following command:

```
$ curl -i -X PUT -H 'Content-Type:text/uri-list' -d http://
localhost:8080/teams/1 localhost:8080/teammates/4/team

HTTP/1.1 204 No Content

Server: Apache-Coyote/1.1
```

We can see a 204 No Content response in the preceding console output. This indicates that the operation was successful, but there is simply no other data to send back.

> As mentioned previously, PATCH updates parts of a resource while PUT completely replaces a resource. You might think that changing a relationship would require using a PATCH, but the semantics are that we are replacing the whole team relationship, so we must use PUT.

After performing the update, let's check Dave's team link, shown as follows:

```
$ curl localhost:8080/teammates/4/team
{
  "name" : "Spring Boot Badgers",
  "_links" : {
    "self" : {
      "href" : "http://localhost:8080/teams/1"
    },
    "members" : {
      "href" : "http://localhost:8080/teams/1/members"
    }
  }
}
```

Previously, we saw 404 Not Found. Now, we can see that Dave is a member of the Spring Boot Badgers. To double-check, it's left as an exercise to look up the members of the team and confirm that Dave is now listed.

To show how to alter a property that isn't a relationship, let's change Dave's position from catcher to short stop:

```
$ curl -i -X PATCH -H "Content-Type:application/json" -d
'{"position":"short stop"}' localhost:8080/teammates/4

HTTP/1.1 204 No Content

Server: Apache-Coyote/1.1

Date: Sun, 03 Aug 2014 02:30:04 GMT
```

Using curl, the preceding command sent a PATCH request with an updated team position. The server responded with `204 No Content`, again indicating success but with no extra data.

To see the results, look at the following command:

```
$ curl localhost:8080/teammates/4
{
  "firstName" : "Dave",
  "lastName" : "Syer",
  "position" : "short stop",
  "_links" : {
    "self" : {
      "href" : "http://localhost:8080/teammates/4"
    },
    "team" : {
      "href" : "http://localhost:8080/teammates/4/team"
    }
  }
}
```

The output clearly shows us that we successfully updated Dave to the position of short stop.

> You might have noticed that the entity's `id` field is not displayed. This is because such a field is internal to the database and not subject to RESTful interactions. The `self` link of an entity is its canonical reference. Why do we need `self`? We might have reached the resource through different relationships. This is the resource's proper identity free of relational context.

As a final step, what if Roy decided to move out of the area and leave our network of teammates? We can easily delete him using the following DELETE command:

```
$ curl -i -X DELETE localhost:8080/teammates/2
HTTP/1.1 204 No Content
Server: Apache-Coyote/1.1
Date: Sun, 03 Aug 2014 02:45:02 GMT
```

```
$ curl -i localhost:8080/teammates/2
HTTP/1.1 404 Not Found
Server: Apache-Coyote/1.1
Content-Length: 0
Date: Sun, 03 Aug 2014 02:45:20 GMT
```

The console output shows us how we executed the DELETE command. We again got a 204 HTTP status code, indicating success. Performing another GET for the same URI shows a 404 error, indicating it no longer exists, as expected.

So, what have we accomplished? We created a RESTful service using Spring Data REST. We didn't have to define Spring view resolvers, message converters, MVC endpoints, hypermedia links, backend database manipulations, and much more. By not having to work on building the endpoints as well as the hypermedia links, we can focus our efforts on a sophisticated frontend instead. There are, in fact, many useful libraries that speak HATEOAS as well as HAL, such as CujoJS's REST library (https://github.com/cujojs/rest).

> For reasons of space, we won't build a UI in this chapter. To see an example that demonstrates Spring Data REST combined with a JavaScript frontend, check out Spring-a-Gram (https://github.com/gregturn/spring-a-gram).

Reconfiguring our app to use Spring Data MongoDB

Up until this point, we have used two relational databases to craft a teammate management app. To wrap up this chapter, we'll investigate how easy it is to retool our app to use MongoDB.

> To install MongoDB on your development machine, downloads are available at http://www.mongodb.org/downloads. Assuming that you have installed MongoDB and started it, proceed with the rest of this section. As a side note, anecdotal evidence suggests that it is important to install the 64-bit version of MongoDB to reduce the risk of data drops in case your data set grows big.

To start things off, we need to revise `build.gradle` so that it contains the following list of dependencies:

```
dependencies {
    compile("org.springframework.boot:spring-boot-starter-data-
    mongodb")
    compile("org.springframework.boot:spring-boot-starter-data-
    rest")
}
```

Using `spring-boot-starter-data-mongodb` and `spring-boot-starter-data-rest`, we will nicely set things up to create a simple app. It's important to note that H2 and MySQL dependencies have been removed. There is no practical reason to use a relational database in development and MongoDB in production. Instead, we can run a tiny MongoDB server on our development workstation while hosting a bigger, more fault-tolerant system in production. We'll see later in this section how to switch between the two.

The following section shows a tweaked snippet of our `Team` domain object:

```
import org.springframework.data.annotation.Id;
import org.springframework.data.mongodb.core.mapping.DBRef;
import org.springframework.data.mongodb.core.mapping.Document;

@Document()
public class Team {

    @Id
    private BigInteger id;

    private String name;

    @DBRef
    private List<Teammate> members;
```

The domain object has the same attributes, but there are a few changes, which are listed as follows:

- The `javax.persistence` imports have been replaced by `org.springframework.data` imports.

- The class itself is tagged by the `@Document` annotation. This annotation is not technically required, but it provides nice documentation. The default name of the collection is the name of the class changed to start with a lowercase letter. The `@Document` annotation has a parameter that changes the name of the collection, if desired.

- The `id` attribute is now annotated by Spring Data Commons' `@Id` annotation. It has also been changed from `Long` to `BigInteger`. (Spring Data MongoDB supports `BigInteger`, `String`, and `ObjectId` for autogenerated ID values.)

- The members attributes have been changed from `@OneToMany` to `@DBRef`. The `@DBRef` annotation indicates that the collection is stored in a separate MongoDB collection instead of being nested directly inside `teams`. Nonetheless, any access to this attribute will render data as if the teammates were stored directly inside its team.

Looking at our other domain object, which is `Teammate`, we can see the same alterations as follows:

```
import org.springframework.data.annotation.Id;
import org.springframework.data.mongodb.core.mapping.Document;

@Document
public class Teammate {

    @Id
    private BigInteger id;

    private String firstName;
    private String lastName;
    private String position;

    private BigInteger teamId;
```

There is one key difference shown in the preceding code: the `@ManyToOne Team team` attribute has been replaced with `BigInteger teamId`. Why was this necessary? MongoDB doesn't directly support bidirectional relationships, nor does it have joins. If we tried to plug in `@DBRef Team team`, any attempt to access a given teammate will result in a stack overflow due to the circular loop that cross-linking would generate. A common way of hedging this circumstance is to manually maintain a copy of the ID, which is what we are doing.

Due to the change of ID types from `Long` to `BigInteger`, we are forced to slightly alter our repositories. Thankfully, that's all we need to edit, considering they are already decoupled from any JPA specifics:

```
public interface TeamRepository extends CrudRepository<Team,
BigInteger> {}
```

The only line that changed is shown in the preceding line. This was applied to our
`TeammateRepository` as well:

```
public interface TeammateRepository extends
CrudRepository<Teammate, BigInteger> {}
```

This preceding repository also shows us moving from `Long` to `BigInteger`. Apart
from this, Spring Data conveniently lets us shift to MongoDB with little effort, as
we'll soon discover. Another part of these slight alterations is our development
environment loader, shown as follows:

```
package learningspringboot;

import javax.annotation.PostConstruct;

import java.util.Arrays;

import org.springframework.beans.factory.annotation.Autowired;
import org.springframework.context.annotation.Profile;
import org.springframework.stereotype.Service;

@Service
@Profile("!production")
public class DatabaseLoader {

    private final TeammateRepository teammateRepository;
    private final TeamRepository teamRepository;

    @Autowired
    public DatabaseLoader(TeammateRepository teammateRepository,
    TeamRepository teamRepository) {
        this.teammateRepository = teammateRepository;
        this.teamRepository = teamRepository;
    }

    @PostConstruct
    private void initDatabase() {
        teamRepository.deleteAll();
        teammateRepository.deleteAll();

        Team springBootTeam = new Team("Spring Boot Badgers");
        teamRepository.save(springBootTeam);
```

```
        Teammate greg = new Teammate("Greg", "Turnquist");
        greg.setPosition("2nd base");
        greg.setTeamId(springBootTeam.getId());
        teammateRepository.save(greg);

        Teammate roy = new Teammate("Roy", "Clarkson");
        roy.setPosition("1st base");
        roy.setTeamId(springBootTeam.getId());
        teammateRepository.save(roy);

        Teammate phil = new Teammate("Phil", "Webb");
        phil.setPosition("pitcher");
        phil.setTeamId(springBootTeam.getId());
        teammateRepository.save(phil);

        springBootTeam.setMembers(Arrays.asList(new Teammate[]{greg,
roy, phil}));
        teamRepository.save(springBootTeam);
    }

}
```

As was the case previously, the DatabaseLoader code is not JPA-specific. It leans on the Spring Data Commons standard API for POJO persistence. This code is still profiled to get activated only if we are not running in a production profile. It also loads up copies of the repositories automatically. The differences are in the initDatabase method as follows:

- As MongoDB persists data between runs, we first need to use deleteAll for both repositories. Otherwise, we'll add new entries every time. This operation is something that should never be used in production, but it's perfect for development.

- Previously, each teammate performed setTeam(springBootTeam). This has been replaced with setTeamId(springBootTeam.getId()). Note that we also added getId to Team in order to support this operation.

- Finally, the one-to-many relationship has to be set up on the team side as well. The setMembers(...) method followed by teamRepository. save(springBootTeam) is required to create this linkage on the team side of things.

In the previous version of our app, we had `application-production.properties` contain production-specific configuration settings. In general, we don't need this file anymore for the following reasons:

- Data is persistent between restarts. When we run with `SPRING_PROFILES_ACTIVE=production`, the `DatabaseLoader` class won't be invoked to prevent data reloads.

- MongoDB is a schema-less system, so the `spring.jpa.hibernate.ddl-auto` property that let us declare `create-drop`, `validate` and `none` is not needed.

The exception would be if our production MongoDB configuration is different from the default configuration. If we get into replication (http://docs.mongodb.org/manual/core/replication-introduction/) or sharding (http://docs.mongodb.org/manual/core/sharding-introduction/), we might very well have to change the connection URI and port. While we won't go into such advanced configuration details here, the following settings are pluggable straight from Spring Boot:

```
spring.data.mongodb.host= # the db host
spring.data.mongodb.port=27017 # the connection port
spring.data.mongodb.uri=mongodb://localhost/test # connection URL
spring.data.mongo.repositories.enabled=true # if SD enabled
```

This listing shows us the default values Spring Boot uses with Spring Data MongoDB. However, we can easily override these values in an `application-${profile}.properties` file for more advanced options.

 Simply having `spring-boot-starter-data-mongodb` is enough to switch on `spring.data.mongo.repositories.enabled`.

As the final step of cleanup, it's advisable to remove the `hibernate` logger setting from `logback.xml`, as follows:

```xml
<?xml version="1.0" encoding="UTF-8"?>
<configuration>
    <include
    resource="org/springframework/boot/logging/logback/base.xml"/>
    <logger name="org.springframework.data.rest" level="DEBUG"/>
</configuration>
```

This is again set up with Spring Boot's default log settings while adding debug logging for Spring Data REST.

Running our MongoDB-based app

With these changes, we can rerun our app in the development mode:

```
$ ./gradlew bootRun
...
2014-08-03 23:46:26.938 ... : Server initialized with port: 8080
2014-08-03 23:46:27.118 ... : Starting service Tomcat
2014-08-03 23:46:27.119 ... : Starting Servlet Engine: Apache
Tomcat/7.0.54
2014-08-03 23:46:27.234 ... : Initializing Spring embedded
WebApplicationContext
2014-08-03 23:46:27.234 ... : Root WebApplicationContext: initialization
compl...
2014-08-03 23:46:28.548 ... : Mapping servlet: 'dispatcherServlet' to [/]
2014-08-03 23:46:28.551 ... : Mapping filter: 'hiddenHttpMethodFilter'
to: [/*]
2014-08-03 23:46:28.759 ... : 2595692249835233023249256838 3: Greg
Turnquist is...
2014-08-03 23:46:28.759 ... : 2595692249835233023249256838 4: Roy Clarkson
is p...
2014-08-03 23:46:28.759 ... : 2595692249835233023249256838 5: Phil Webb is
play...
...
```

The preceding console output has been trimmed to show that our teammates—Greg, Roy, and Phil—have very different IDs. They are big integers. Everything else was the same, so it was cut out for space reasons.

We can query for the list of teams again, shown as follows:

```
$ curl localhost:8080/teams
{
  "_embedded" : {
    "teams" : [ {
      "id" : 2595692249835233023249256838 2,
      "name" : "Spring Boot Badgers",
      "members" : [ {
        "firstName" : "Greg",
        "lastName" : "Turnquist",
```

```
      "position" : "2nd base",
      "teamId" : 2595692249835233023249256838382
    }, {
      "firstName" : "Roy",
      "lastName" : "Clarkson",
      "position" : "1st base",
      "teamId" : 2595692249835233023249256838382
    }, {
      "firstName" : "Phil",
      "lastName" : "Webb",
      "position" : "pitcher",
      "teamId" : 2595692249835233023249256838382
    } ],
    "_links" : {
      "self" : {
        "href" : "http://localhost:8080/
teams/2595692249835233023249256838382"
      },
      "members" : {
        "href" : "http://localhost:8080/
teams/2595692249835233023249256838382/members"
      }
    }
  } ]
  }
}
```

This shows us the Spring Boot Badgers, which we saw previously. Apart from having different IDs, what is different in the preceding printout? Take a look:

- In the previous version of our app, members was only listed underneath _links. In this situation, not only is there a link but we also see our teammates being displayed directly.

- We can see the new teamId property for each teammate. It matches the enclosing team's id.

Now, let's look directly at the list of teammates, as follows:

```
$ curl localhost:8080/teammates
{
  "_embedded" : {
    "teammates" : [ {
      "firstName" : "Greg",
      "lastName" : "Turnquist",
      "position" : "2nd base",
      "teamId" : 259569224983523302324925683382,
      "_links" : {
        "self" : {
          "href" : "http://localhost:8080/
teammates/259569224983523302324925683383"
        }
      }
    }, {
      "firstName" : "Roy",
      "lastName" : "Clarkson",
      "position" : "1st base",
      "teamId" : 259569224983523302324925683382,
      "_links" : {
        "self" : {
          "href" : "http://localhost:8080/
teammates/259569224983523302324925683384"
        }
      }
    }, {
      "firstName" : "Phil",
      "lastName" : "Webb",
      "position" : "pitcher",
      "teamId" : 259569224983523302324925683382,
      "_links" : {
        "self" : {
          "href" : "http://localhost:8080/
teammates/259569224983523302324925683385"
        }
      }
    } ]
  }
}
```

This output is very similar to the previous output, except that it also lists relevant links for each teammate. A key difference between our MongoDB version and the JPA-based version is that there is no official link to the team. We can see `teamId`, but it requires semantic knowledge of the domain classes.

 Does managing `teamId` without a corresponding hypermedia link violate the principles of REST? Arguably so. However, given MongoDB's lack of normalized relationships, it's a compromise that can be deemed suitable, given the chance that MongoDB might be a faster, more scalable solution for certain problems.

All the other RESTful operations work as before, so we won't repeat them here. This should show us how easy it is to decouple our app from the underlying datastore.

Summary

In this chapter, we created an app to manage teams and teammates. We preloaded it with one team and three players and stored it in a relational, in-memory database. This was good for development purposes. Then, we created a separate profile targeting production and pointed our app towards a standalone MySQL database. With this profile, we disabled schema creation and data loading, leaving the production database intact. Finally, we switched our database to the NoSQL datastore MongoDB.

For reasons of space, we used Spring Data REST instead of creating a web frontend. It provided us with a powerful, hypermedia-driven way to interact with the content. We mentioned how this API combined with CujoJS's REST library can very easily be used to build a web page in lieu of server-side templates.

In the next chapter, we will examine how to secure a Spring Boot application quickly, customizing and overriding Boot's opinion as required.

5
Securing Your App with Spring Boot

"The real benefit of Boot, however, is that it's just Spring. That means any direction the code takes, regardless of complexity, I know it's a safe bet. I don't worry about my code scaling. Boot allows the developer to peel back the layers and customize when it's appropriate while keeping the conventions that just work."

— Jeff Taggart

In the previous chapter, we learned how to access different data stores using Spring Boot. We also figured out how to configure different profiles so that we develop against one system while maintaining another.

In this chapter, we will be:

- Creating a teammate management app
- Adding Spring Security and seeing how Spring Boot automatically locks down all HTTP endpoints
- Configuring different levels of protection for different endpoints
- Plugging in a prebuilt set of user accounts
- Configuring the authentication manager to use a persistent database for user data storage
- Configuring the embedded Tomcat servlet engine to use SSL

Getting started

We are going to start this chapter by creating a fully functional Spring MVC app that is used to manage a roster of teammates. This is very similar to the app we built in *Chapter 4, Data Access with Spring Boot*, but it is simplified a bit. Then we will apply security settings.

First of all, we need to set up a Gradle project. Using `http://start.spring.io` (or working on our own), we can construct the following `build.gradle` file:

```
buildscript {
    repositories {
        mavenCentral()
    }
    dependencies {
        classpath("org.springframework.boot:spring-boot-gradle-
        plugin:1.1.6.RELEASE")
    }
}

apply plugin: 'java'
apply plugin: 'spring-boot'

jar {
    baseName = 'teams'
    version =   '0.0.1-SNAPSHOT'
}
sourceCompatibility = 1.8
targetCompatibility = 1.8

repositories {
    mavenCentral()
}


dependencies {
    compile("org.springframework.boot:spring-boot-starter-
    thymeleaf")
    compile("org.springframework.boot:spring-boot-starter-
    data-jpa")
    compile("org.springframework.hateoas:spring-hateoas")
    compile("com.h2database:h2")
}
task wrapper(type: Wrapper) {
    gradleVersion = '2.1'
}
```

Let's review some key settings listed here:

- The preceding file uses `spring-boot-gradle-plugin` so that we can build, package, and run Spring Boot apps
- The project is configured to use Java 8 for both source input and target output
- It includes support for the Gradle wrapper

The included dependencies are as follows:

Dependency	Description
`spring-boot-starter-thymeleaf`	Pulls in Spring MVC, Thymeleaf template engine, Jackson 2 JSON support, and embedded Tomcat
`spring-boot-starter-data-jpa`	Spring Data JPA
`spring-hateoas`	Spring HATEOAS for hypermedia links
`h2`	H2 in-memory database

With this in place, we are ready to craft our teammate app.

Defining our domain

Let's bring in the domain model from the previous chapter but with a slight alteration. Let's define a single teammate:

```
package learningspringboot;

import javax.persistence.Entity;
import javax.persistence.GeneratedValue;
import javax.persistence.Id;

@Entity
public class Teammate {

    @Id @GeneratedValue private Long id;

    private String firstName;
    private String lastName;
    private String position;

    protected Teammate() {}
```

```java
    public Teammate(String firstName, String lastName) {
        this();
        this.firstName = firstName;
        this.lastName = lastName;
    }

    public Long getId() {
        return id;
    }

    public void setId(Long id) { this.id = id; }

    public String getFirstName() {
        return firstName;
    }

    public void setFirstName(String firstName) {
        this.firstName = firstName;
    }

    public String getLastName() {
        return lastName;
    }

    public void setLastName(String lastName) {
        this.lastName = lastName;
    }

    public String getPosition() {
        return position;
    }

    public void setPosition(String position) {
        this.position = position;
    }

    @Override
    public String toString() {
        return id + ": " + firstName + " " + lastName + " is
        playing " + position;
    }
}
```

Let break down this domain object:

- Each player has `firstName`, `lastName`, and `position`.

- The publicly visible constructor requires a first and last name. This implies that the position isn't required to define a teammate.

- Each field has a getter and a setter as well.

- We had to provide an empty, default constructor that supports conventional JPA requirements. We set its visibility to protected in order to discourage developers from using it directly.

- There is a custom `toString` method to print out a player and their position on the team.

> *Chapter 4, Data Access with Spring Boot,* had a two-table structure. This chapter has trimmed things back to a single table in order to lighten the controllers and templates required to build a fully functioning web app. This way, we can spend more time focused on security-specific details.

This nice little one-table JPA structure provides a simple problem space for this chapter: managing teammates. The most effective way for our app to interact with this table is using the full force of Spring Data JPA (`http://projects.spring.io/spring-data-jpa`). To do this, we need to create a repository interface for `Teammate`:

```
package learningspringboot;

import org.springframework.data.repository.CrudRepository;

public interface TeammateRepository extends
CrudRepository<Teammate, Long> {}
```

The preceding interface might appear empty, but the inherited methods inside `CrudRepository` provide the core CRUD operations we need, including `save`, `findOne`, `findAll`, `delete`, `exists`, and `count`. The interface is generically typed to match up with the domain class and the ID's field type.

With this code in place, when Spring Boot creates an application context, Spring Data JPA will scan and discover our repository definition. Then it will automatically generate a concrete proxy that implements this interface. This saves us the labor of writing all these queries. For more details about this process, reread *Chapter 4, Data Access with Spring Boot.*

Loading the test data

With this repository, we are now ready to preload some teammate data. To do this, let's create a database-loading service:

```
package learningspringboot;

import javax.annotation.PostConstruct;

import org.springframework.beans.factory.annotation.Autowired;
import org.springframework.stereotype.Service;

@Service
public class DatabaseLoader {

    private final TeammateRepository teammateRepository;

    @Autowired
    public DatabaseLoader(TeammateRepository teammateRepository) {
        this.teammateRepository = teammateRepository;
    }

    @PostConstruct
    private void initDatabase() {
        Teammate roy = new Teammate("Roy", "Clarkson");
        roy.setPosition("1st base");
        teammateRepository.save(roy);

        Teammate phil = new Teammate("Phil", "Webb");
        phil.setPosition("pitcher");
        teammateRepository.save(phil);

    }
}
```

Let's look into the database loader class:

- The `DatabaseLoader` class is annotated at the class level with `@Service`, which means that it will be automatically picked up and instantiated by Spring.
- It uses constructor injection and autowiring to load a copy of Spring Data JPA's concrete implementation of `TeammateRepository`.
- The `@PostConstruct` annotation tells Spring to invoke `initDatabase` after all beans have been created. This will conveniently use the Spring Data repository to load up two players.

Preloading data is only for development and demo purposes.
This type of code should not be used in a real production app.
Even though this chapter will define a **production** environment,
it is still just a demo in this book.

Creating a server-side controller

Next, we need to create the Spring MVC web layer:

```java
package learningspringboot;

import static org.springframework.hateoas.mvc.ControllerLinkBuilder.*;

import java.util.Arrays;
import java.util.stream.StreamSupport;

import org.springframework.beans.factory.annotation.Autowired;
import org.springframework.stereotype.Controller;
import org.springframework.web.bind.annotation.ModelAttribute;
import org.springframework.web.bind.annotation.PathVariable;
import org.springframework.web.bind.annotation.RequestMapping;
import org.springframework.web.bind.annotation.RequestMethod;
import org.springframework.web.servlet.ModelAndView;

@Controller
public class TeammateController {

    private final TeammateRepository teammateRepository;

    @Autowired
    public TeammateController(TeammateRepository
    teammateRepository) {
        this.teammateRepository = teammateRepository;
    }

    @RequestMapping(value = "/teammates", method =
    RequestMethod.GET)
    public ModelAndView getTeammates() {
        // Specify the view name
        return new ModelAndView("teammates")
            // Look up ALL teammates and wrap each with
            related links
```

```
        .addObject("teammates",
            StreamSupport.stream(teammateRepository.
                findAll().spliterator(), false)
                .map(TeammateAndLink::new)
                .toArray())
        // new Teammate command object
        .addObject("teammate", new Teammate())
        .addObject("postLink",
            linkTo(methodOn(TeammateController.class)
                .newTeammate(null))
                .withRel("Create"))
        .addObject("links", Arrays.asList(
            linkTo(methodOn(TeammateController.class)
                .getTeammates())
                .withRel("All Teammates")
        ));
    }


    @RequestMapping(value = "/teammates", method =
    RequestMethod.POST)
    public ModelAndView newTeammate(@ModelAttribute Teammate
    teammate) {
        // Save the newly created teammate
        teammateRepository.save(teammate);
        // Return the All Teammates page
        return getTeammates();
    }


    @RequestMapping(value = "/teammate/{id}", method =
    RequestMethod.GET)
    public ModelAndView getTeammate(@PathVariable Long id) {
        // Look up the related teammate
        final Teammate teammate = teammateRepository.findOne(id);
        return new ModelAndView("teammate")
            .addObject("teammate", teammate)
            .addObject("links", Arrays.asList(
                linkTo(methodOn(TeammateController.class).
                    getTeammates())
                    .withRel("All Teammates"),
                linkTo(methodOn(TeammateController.class)
                    .editTeammate(id))
                    .withRel("Edit")
            ));
    }
```

```
@RequestMapping(value = "/teammate/{id}", method =
RequestMethod.PUT)
public ModelAndView updateTeammate(@PathVariable Long id,
                                   @ModelAttribute Teammate
                                   teammate)
{
    // Connect the new teammate info with the PUT {id}
    teammate.setId(id);
    teammateRepository.save(teammate);
    // Return the teammate view
    return getTeammate(teammate.getId());
}


@RequestMapping(value = "/teammate/{id}/edit", method =
RequestMethod.GET)
public ModelAndView editTeammate(@PathVariable Long id) {
    final Teammate teammate = teammateRepository.findOne(id);
    return new ModelAndView("edit")
        .addObject("teammate", teammate)
        .addObject("putLink",
            linkTo(methodOn(TeammateController.class)
                .updateTeammate(id, teammate))
                .withRel("Update"))
        .addObject("links", Arrays.asList(
            linkTo(methodOn(TeammateController.class)
                .getTeammate(id))
                .withRel("Cancel")
        ));
}

}
```

There is a quite a bit of power packed into this single controller class. Let's look
into it:

- The entire class is marked with `@Controller`. This ensures that the class is
  automatically loaded into the application context and is also used by Spring
  MVC for web requests.

- Once again, we use constructor injection and autowiring to ensure that the
  controller has a copy of `TeammateRepository`.

- Each method has a similar pattern. A `@RequestMapping` annotation defines
  the route and HTTP verb it responds to. The return type is `ModelAndView`,
  which contains the name of the view as well as parameters for the
  view template.

This Spring MVC controller responds to several GET calls, a POST call that creates a new teammate, and a PUT call that updates an existing one. The key is that each page yields not only some information, such as teammate info, but also includes relevant links.

 This controller does have a class called `TeammateAndLink`. If you have been coding step by step, you are probably getting a compiler error. The purpose of this class will be shown right after the upcoming table.

To provide proper links, this app uses Spring HATEOAS (`http://projects.spring.io/spring-hateoas`).

 HATEOAS (Hypermedia As The Engine Of Application State) is part of Roy Fielding's REST thesis. It essentially says that a RESTful API should also include links that describe the relevant transitions for a given resource. Spring HATEOAS makes it super simple to create links to Spring MVC controller methods. For more details, you can read his REST thesis at `http://www.ics.uci.edu/~fielding/pubs/dissertation/top.htm`.

Now, let's break down each method of this controller with the following table:

Method	HTTP Verb	Route	Details
getTeammates	GET	/teammates	The view name is `teammates`. It displays all teammates and runs through a Java 8 stream, mapping each team into `TeammateAndLink`, which is described later. It also includes an empty `Teammate` class to support the option to create new teammates. It includes links to `newTeammate` and `getTeammates`.
newTeammate	POST	/teammates	The `@ModelAttribute` annotation signals Spring MVC to extract `Teammate` from the body of the POST and marshal it for this method. It saves it using `TeammateRepository`. Then it returns `getTeammates`.

Method	HTTP Verb	Route	Details
getTeammate	GET	/teammate/{id}	The @PathVariable annotation extracts {id} from the URL so that it can fetch a single Teammate object using the repository. The view name is teammate. It returns the teammate along with links to getTeammates and editTeammate.
updateTeammate	PUT	/teammate/{id}	The @PathVariable annotation extracts {id}. The @ModelAttribute annotation signals Spring MVC to extract Teammate from the body of the POST and marshal it for this method. A new Teammate object is configured to use id and is then saved using the repository. The freshly stored teammate is returned using getTeammate(id).
editTeammate	GET	/teammate/{id}/edit	The @PathVariable annotation extracts {id}. The view name is edit. It uses the repository to fetch Teammate based on id. It embeds the object into a template parameter. It also includes links to updateTeammate and getTeammate.

An important concept is that when rendering a list of teammates, each teammate entry needs its own link to its respective /teammate/{id} controller method. Instead of trying to embed a link to a controller method inside the Teammate domain object, we should create a container, which is TeammateAndLink. The getTeammates method uses a simple Java 8 stream/map operation to iterate over the entire List<Teammate>, map each item onto TeammateAndLink::new, and subsequently, create a List<TeammateAndLink>, which is shown as follows:

```
package learningspringboot;

import static
org.springframework.hateoas.mvc.ControllerLinkBuilder.*;
```

```
import org.springframework.hateoas.Link;

public class TeammateAndLink {

    private final Teammate teammate;
    private final Link link;

    public TeammateAndLink(Teammate teammate) {
        this.teammate = teammate;
        this.link = linkTo(methodOn(TeammateController.class)
                .getTeammate(teammate.getId()))
                .withRel(teammate.getFirstName() + " " +
                teammate.getLastName());
    }

    public Teammate getTeammate() {
        return teammate;
    }

    public Link getLink() {
        return link;
    }
}
```

This class is a container. We create an instance using a constructor call, not setters. This means that the internal data won't change. The only way to change the data is to create a new instance.

The constructor stores the `Teammate` instance in the `teammate` field. Then, it creates a `Link` to the controller's `getTeammate()` method with the `teammate`'s id value plugged in. It also assigns the link a rel of `<firstname> <lastname>`. This way, link creation is decoupled from the `Teammate` record itself, granting us flexibility in changing the link structure later on.

What are rels? In hypermedia, a rel or relation is the logical name associated with the URI. The concept is that we shouldn't be tightly coupling clients to RESTful services by hardcoding URIs into the UI. Instead, we should use rels to interrogate the hypermedia, providing a fluid way for URIs to change without impacting the client, if need be.

Crafting our HTML templates

With the controller defined, we can now work on the templates. We'll go through them in the same order in which they were defined in the controller earlier.

The first template we need is one that lists all the players on the roster. Create `src/main/resources/templates/teammates.html` as follows:

```html
<html xmlns:th="http://www.thymeleaf.org">
<head>
    <title>Learning Spring Boot - Chapter 5</title>
</head>
<body>
    <h2>All Teammates</h2>

    <ul>
        <li th:each="t : ${teammates}">
            <a th:href="${t.link.href}"
               th:text="${t.teammate.firstName} + ' ' +
               ${t.teammate.lastName} + ' plays ' +
               ${t.teammate.position}"/>
        </li>
    </ul>

    <h2>Create a new teammate</h2>

    <form th:action="${postLink.href}" th:object="${teammate}"
    method="post">
        <input type="text" th:field="*{firstName}" />
        <input type="text" th:field="*{lastName}" />
        <input type="text" th:field="*{position}" />
        <input type="submit" />
    </form>

    <div th:include="_links :: nav"/>
</body>
</html>
```

Let's break down this template:

- The template contains a complete web page.
- It has a header, which indicates that it lists All Teammates.
- There is an unordered list (`<ul>`), which contains a Thymeleaf `for-each` loop to generate a series of line items (`<li>`).

- Inside each line item, there is an anchor element (`<a>`) that points at that row's `Link.getHref()` statement.

- The text value of the anchor element is a concatenation of the teammate's first name, last name, and position. Notice how the whole `th:text` attribute is enclosed in double quotes, while each segment is either `${some attribute}` or a raw string value wrapped in single quotes and joined with +.

- Later, there is a form (`<form>`) for creating a new teammate using the `teammate` attribute.

- At the bottom is a fragment that is used to render any and all links supplied by the controller (which we'll explore later on in this section).

Whew! That seems like a lot, but it's a power-packed template. Don't forget that in this template `teammates` is an instance of `TeammateAndLink`. It makes it easy to access each individual teammate's properties and the associated link. Did you also notice that there are no hardcoded paths to the server-side controller? This is because we carefully embedded them as various attributes using Spring HATEOAS.

Next, we need to code a template that inspects a single teammate at `src/main/resources/templates/teammate.html`:

```
<html xmlns:th="http://www.thymeleaf.org">
<head>
    <title>Learning Spring Boot - Chapter 5</title>
</head>
<body>
    <h2 th:text="${teammate.firstName} + ' ' +
    ${teammate.lastName}" />
    <h3 th:text="'Plays ' + ${teammate.position}" />

    <div th:include="_links :: nav"/>
</body>
</html>
```

This template is a bit simpler. It shows you the person and the position he or she plays, wrapped in level 2 and 3 header elements. It also includes the same Thymeleaf fragment of links to be displayed at the bottom of the page.

We also need a page to edit existing players, so let's create `src/main/resources/templates/edit.html`, which is shown as follows:

```
<html xmlns:th="http://www.thymeleaf.org">
<head>
    <title>Learning Spring Boot - Chapter 5</title>
</head>
```

```
<body>
    <h2>Edit a teammate</h2>

    <form th:action="${putLink.href}" th:object="${teammate}"
    th:method="put">
        <input type="text" th:field="*{firstName}" />
        <input type="text" th:field="*{lastName}" />
        <input type="text" th:field="*{position}" />
        <input type="submit" />
    </form>

    <div th:include="_links :: nav"/>
</body>
</html>
```

There is a bit more complexity to this form, so let's break it down:

- We use a conventional `<form>` element but use `th:action="${putLink.href}"` to insert the URI supplied from the controller via Spring HATEOAS.

- The `th:object=${teammate}` attribute indicates that this is a bean-backed form, that is, a command object and that the `teammate` attribute sent over from the server is the object we intend to populate.

- HTML only supports GET and POST. The form in `teammates.html` only needed `method="post"`. In order to use the HTTP verb PUT, we must use `th:method="put"`. Notice the `th` prefix. This causes Thymeleaf to add an extra hidden parameter that Spring MVC will use to decode the method on the server side. It's still a POST as far as HTTP is concerned, but Spring MVC will turn it into PUT on the server.

- Each of the input fields has `th:field="*{attributeName}"`, such that `attributeName` is an attribute of the `teammate` object.

- This template also pulls in the same fragment to render links at the bottom of the page.

These three templates define the three web pages in our app. To top things off, we must also create the `src/main/resources/templates/_links.html` Thymeleaf fragment, which is shown as follows:

```
<html xmlns:th="http://www.thymeleaf.org">

<div th:fragment="nav">
    <h3>Links:</h3>
    <ul>
```

```
        <li th:each="link : ${links}">
            <a th:href="${link.href}" th:text="${link.rel}"/>
        </li>
    </ul>
</div>

</html>
```

This chunk of HTML isn't intended to be displayed as a whole web page. Instead, it simply wraps everything inside an `<html>` element. From there, each fragment is essentially a division element (`<div>`). In this case, we have a header that shows `Links:` followed by an unordered list (`<ul>`). It then uses a Thymeleaf `for-each` loop to create a separate line item (`<li>`), displaying each link's `rel` attribute linked to `href`.

This fragment provides a nice generalized way to display all links. This allows us to contain the actual link formation inside the controller and not have to fiddle with it in the client.

If you'll notice, the links for the forms and the fragment at the bottom are supplied by the controller. This makes it possible for us to keep link management inside the Java code where we can leverage Spring HATEOAS. This way, there is only one place where we have to define a route, and that place is inside a given `@RequestMapping` annotation. This way, if we rename a method or alter its route, the compiler will detect any mistakes and automatically adjust the generated HTML suitably.

With everything set up, we just need an `Application` class to launch everything. If you used `http://start.spring.io`, a class has already been created for you. Otherwise, create one as follows:

```
package learningspringboot;

import org.springframework.boot.SpringApplication;
import
org.springframework.boot.autoconfigure.EnableAutoConfiguration;
import org.springframework.context.annotation.ComponentScan;

@ComponentScan
@EnableAutoConfiguration
public class Application {

    public static void main(String[] args) {
        SpringApplication.run(Application.class, args);
    }
}
```

This should be a familiar pattern by now. It has the familiar `@ComponentScan` annotation so that it will find the `DatabaseLoader` service and the `TeammateController` class. It will also automatically configure everything thanks to `@EnableAutoConfiguration`.

 Even though `http://start.spring.io` will also annotate this class with `@Configuration`, it's not necessary as there are no beans defined in this class.

Running our unsecured application

It's important to point out that nothing has been secured yet. Instead, let's first get familiar with our app. Time to fire things up! Take a look at this command:

```
$ ./gradlew bootRun
```

 You might not see `bootRun` ever reach 100 percent and yet be reachable. This could be a quirk in `spring-boot-gradle-plugin`. Don't worry about it.

Now, with our browser, let's visit the list of teams at `http://localhost:8080/teammates`.

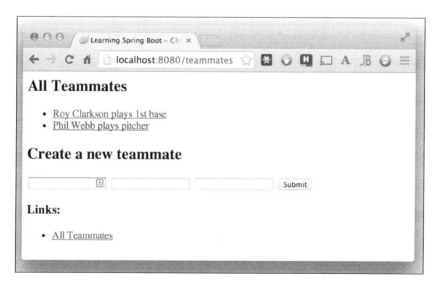

What can be seen in this snapshot of our browser? Take a look:

- We see Roy and Phil listed with hyperlinks
- We can enter the details of a new player
- Finally, there is an **All Teammates** link, which is a proverbial "self" link to the page we are viewing

Let's click on Roy and see what is displayed.

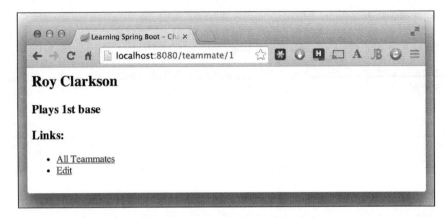

Here, we can see the details about Roy. We have links at the bottom to navigate back to either **All Teammates** or **Edit**. Let's click on **Edit** and change Roy's position.

We have the ability to edit Roy's record. We can change his name or position. At the bottom is a link for **Cancel**, which essentially exits the edit page with no changes. This screenshot shows us about to move Roy to third base. Let's click on **Submit** and make it a done deal.

Roy has now been updated to play third base. Great!

So what do we have? Basically, this is a very simple way to manage a team roster. It's not very fancy, but we have a nice, navigable domain.

> It's important to note that at no time did we manually concatenate strings together to create links between objects. Instead, we let Spring HATEOAS generate links to controller methods. We supplied them to the templates as attributes. This means that if we go back and alter the routes in the controller, we won't have to edit any other code for the links to continue working.
>
> Again, it's important to recognize that this application is completely unsecured. If it was deployed publicly, anyone could visit it and make edits to the team, whether that was authorized or not.

So, let's dive in and apply some security using the speedy power of Spring Boot.

Securing our app

The first step is to pull in `spring-boot-starter-security`. In our Gradle build file, let's update the `dependencies` section to look like the following code:

```
dependencies {
    compile("org.springframework.boot:spring-boot-starter-
    thymeleaf")
    compile("org.springframework.boot:spring-boot-starter-data-
    jpa")
    compile("org.springframework.boot:spring-boot-starter-
    security")
    compile("org.springframework.hateoas:spring-hateoas")
    compile("com.h2database:h2")
}
```

This single line of build configuration will generate a whole host of updates when we run the app again:

- All HTTP endpoints are secured with basic authentication (`http://tools.ietf.org/html/rfc2617`). The username is `user` and the password is randomly generated and printed out to the console.

- A collection of routes are ignored from any security checks including `/css/`, `/js/`, and `/images/`, and `**/favicon.ico`.

- Security events are published to the Spring container regarding successful and unsuccessful authentications and authorization requests.

- Common security headers are activated, including **HSTS (HTTP Strict Transport Security)**, **XSS (Cross-site Scripting)**, **CSRF (Cross-site Request Forgery)**, and **Cache Control** (to prevent users from viewing secured data stored in the browser's cache). Note that this only works if the certificate for your app is trusted by the browser. Self-signed certificates won't work for this.

Here's a quick primer on some of these security headers:

Protocol	Description
HSTS	If you visit a particular page through SSL, the browser will remember and push you to SSL the next time. This is good because it ensures that potentially sensitive data won't be snooped just because the user forget to use the SSL port on subsequent visits. This is often applied when users log in and are switched to HTTPS. Feel free to read the specification at `http://tools.ietf.org/html/rfc6797`.
XSS	Cross-site Scripting is an attack vector whereby client-side code is injected to try and bypass security controls such as access controls or same origin policies. For more details, read `http://docs.spring.io/spring-security/site/docs/current/reference/htmlsingle/#headers-xss-protection`. It should be emphasize that this helps but doesn't completely eliminate XSS risks. It primarily addresses reflected XSS attacks.
CSRF	Cross-site Request Forgery is a more complex attack where a malicious site might attempt to use validated cookies to conduct unauthorized activities. The solution is to embed a randomly generated token value in the form. As a malicious website with a hijacked form won't know the value, it will fail when the form is submitted. For more information, see `http://docs.spring.io/spring-security/site/docs/current/reference/htmlsingle/#csrf`.
Cache Control	Despite logging out of a website, it's possible that a browser will have cached sensitive data. Spring Security embeds extra headers to avoid letting cached data linger after the user has logged out. By the way, if you plug in your own Cache Control header settings, Spring Security will back away and not overwrite your opinion. This comes in handy for things such as static images, CSS, and other resources that we need to get cached.

While a randomly generated password is excellent for demonstrating security, we often wish to switch to a custom password that won't change constantly. To do this, we have to create `src/main/resources/application.properties` as follows:

```
security.user.name=admin
security.user.password=learningspringboot
```

In this example, we also replaced the default username of `user` with `admin`.

Navigating with basic authentication

If we run the app again (either with `./gradlew bootRun` or by running `Application.main`) and visit `http://localhost:8080/teammates`, we can expect to see the following output:

Enter `admin/learningspringboot`, and access will be granted.

> Be aware that the transport layer is completely unsecured. Sending a username or password to an HTTP endpoint does not protect us from people snooping the network. Toward the end of this chapter, we will learn how to configure Spring Boot's embedded Tomcat server to run with SSL.

Let's review the configuration provided by simply adding Spring Security to the classpath:

- The entire site is locked down, requiring username/password access
- No authorization exists; only authentication exists
- Only one account is supplied

In general, this is a handy way to demonstrate security, but it's probably not the most preferred model of security. Others can snoop the network and detect our password. Only having a single account, by definition, doesn't allow multiple users to access the system without sharing an account (something that we highly recommended you avoid).

Enhancing the security model of our app

So far, we've used Spring Boot's default security settings. This means locking down everything with only one account to access things. To customize things in a better manner, we need to create a configuration class with a method using Spring Security's `AuthenticationManagerBuilder` class:

```
package learningspringboot;

import org.springframework.beans.factory.annotation.Autowired;
import org.springframework.context.annotation.Configuration;
import org.springframework.http.HttpMethod;
import org.springframework.security.config.annotation.authentication.
builders.AuthenticationManagerBuilder;
import org.springframework.security.config.annotation.method.
configuration.EnableGlobalMethodSecurity;
import org.springframework.security.config.annotation.web.builders.
HttpSecurity;
import org.springframework.security.config.annotation.web.
configuration.
WebSecurityConfigurerAdapter;

@Configuration
@EnableGlobalMethodSecurity(securedEnabled = true)
public class SecurityConfiguration extends
WebSecurityConfigurerAdapter {

    @Autowired
    public void configureAuth(AuthenticationManagerBuilder auth)
            throws Exception {
        auth.inMemoryAuthentication()
            .withUser("phil").password("webb").roles("USER").and()
            .withUser("roy").password("clarkson").roles("USER",
            "ADMIN");
    }

    @Override
    protected void configure(HttpSecurity http) throws Exception {
        http
            .authorizeRequests()
                .antMatchers(HttpMethod.GET,
                "/teammates").permitAll()
                .anyRequest().authenticated()
                .and()
```

```
            .formLogin()
                .defaultSuccessUrl("/teammates")
                .and()
            .logout()
                .logoutSuccessUrl("/teammates");
    }
}
```

Let's break down this security configuration:

- The `@EnableGlobalMethodSecurity(securedEnabled = true)` annotation switches on Spring Security's method-level security features using its native annotations. This annotation only works on a class marked with `@Configuration`.

- The `configureAuth` method is an autowired method that gives us a handle on Spring Security's `AuthenticationManagerBuilder` instance. This lets us configure `Roy` (ROLE_ADMIN and ROLE_USER) and `Phil` (ROLE_USER) in an in-memory user list while still retaining the rest of Spring Boot's auto-configured Spring Security beans.

- By overriding `WebSecurityConfigurerAdapter.configure`, we are able to define a tailored security policy. Let's explore the details of this policy in the following paragraph.

The `HttpSecurity` class is a fluent API that is meant to provide a lightweight, readable experience similar to Spring Security's older XML-based one. It works by chaining multiple policy settings using `.and()`.

The following table provides more details about each of these options:

Method	Description
`authorizeRequests()`	This clause tells us about the authorization rules to be followed. In this case, `antMatcher(HttpMethod.GET, '/teammates').permitAll()` says that `GET /teammates` requires no authentication. The `anyRequest().authenticated` rule says that any request must be authenticated. As this is after `GET /teammates`, it is the catch-all security rule. See `http://docs.spring.io/spring-security/site/docs/current/reference/htmlsingle/#authorize-requests` for more examples.

Method	Description
`formLogin()`	Turn on Spring Security's default login form. The form itself as well as a login controller is included out of the box, which means that we don't have to create our own. Want to write your own login form? Visit `http://spring.io/guides/gs/securing-web` and you'll see how to create your own form and register it.
`logout()`	This defines that `/logout` will trip a logout action. In this situation, when someone logs out, we are automatically redirecting them to `/teammates` using `logoutSuccessUrl()`. Again, processing a logout request is provided out of the box from Spring Security. We don't have to code a controller method to handle this.

We could have coded more authorization rules inside `SecurityConfiguration`. However, we are using method-level security instead. Let's see how we can do this by going back to `TeammateController` and adding some security settings, which are shown as follows:

```
...
import static
org.springframework.hateoas.mvc.ControllerLinkBuilder.*;

import java.util.ArrayList;
import java.util.Arrays;
import java.util.List;
import java.util.stream.StreamSupport;

import org.springframework.beans.factory.annotation.Autowired;
import org.springframework.hateoas.Link;
import org.springframework.security.access.annotation.Secured;
import
org.springframework.security.core.context.SecurityContextHolder;
...
@Controller
public class TeammateController {
...
    @RequestMapping(value = "/teammates", method =
    RequestMethod.GET)
    public ModelAndView getTeammates() {
        ...
```

```
        }

        @Secured("ROLE_ADMIN")
        @RequestMapping(value = "/teammates", method =
        RequestMethod.POST)
        public ModelAndView newTeammate(@ModelAttribute Teammate
        teammate) {
            ...
        }

        @Secured("ROLE_ADMIN")
        @RequestMapping(value = "/teammate/{id}", method =
        RequestMethod.PUT)
        public ModelAndView updateTeammate(@PathVariable Long id,
                                           @ModelAttribute Teammate
                                                           teammate)
        {
            ...
        }

        @Secured("ROLE_ADMIN")
        @RequestMapping(value = "/teammate/{id}/edit", method =
        RequestMethod.GET)
        public ModelAndView editTeammate(@PathVariable Long id) {
            ...
        }
    }
```

We can quickly discern all the new security settings shown in the preceding code:

- The `@Secured` annotation is used to declare the role required to access a given method

- The `getTeammates` method is not flagged with any role. Instead, it is covered in the security policy with `antMatchers(HttpMethod.GET, "/teammates").permitAll()`. This means that no security is required to fetch a list of teammates. (To be precise, Spring Security grants ROLE_ANONYMOUS, and this is good enough for `getTeammates`.)

- The `newTeammate`, `updateTeammate`, and `editTeammate` methods are flagged to only accept users with ROLE_ADMIN. This ensures that the backend is secured regardless of what HTML options are offered on the frontend.

> Because method-level security is applied via a proxy, only methods invoked externally from a class that is wired as a Spring bean are subject to security checks. One method calling another inside the same class won't incur any additional method checks. If you need additional checks or have beans created outside Spring's DI container, check out http://docs.spring.io/spring-security/site/docs/current/reference/htmlsingle/#aspectj to see what can be applied if you introduce AspectJ to your project.

The one method not discussed in the preceding code is `getTeammate`. This is because it has a slightly different security requirement.

Our application grants the power to edit only to users with ROLE_ADMIN. In this situation, we should only include the link to `editTeammate` if the user has that role. We can't solve this with a method-level security check. Instead, we need something different:

```
import static
org.springframework.hateoas.mvc.ControllerLinkBuilder.*;

import java.util.ArrayList;
import java.util.Arrays;
import java.util.List;
import java.util.stream.StreamSupport;

import org.springframework.beans.factory.annotation.Autowired;
import org.springframework.hateoas.Link;
import org.springframework.security.access.annotation.Secured;
import
org.springframework.security.core.context.SecurityContextHolder;
...
@Controller
public class TeammateController {
...
    @Secured("ROLE_USER")
    @RequestMapping(value = "/teammate/{id}", method =
    RequestMethod.GET)
    public ModelAndView getTeammate(@PathVariable Long id) {
        ModelAndView modelAndView = new ModelAndView("teammate");
        // Look up the related teammate
        final Teammate teammate = teammateRepository.findOne(id);
        modelAndView.addObject("teammate", teammate);
```

```
        List<Link> links = new ArrayList<>();

        links.add(linkTo(methodOn(TeammateController.class).
        getTeammates())
                .withRel("All Teammates"));

        if (SecurityContextHolder.getContext().getAuthentication()
            .getAuthorities().stream().anyMatch(
                p -> p.getAuthority().equals("ROLE_ADMIN"))) {
                links.add(linkTo(methodOn
                (TeammateController.class).editTeammate(id))
                    .withRel("Edit"));
        }

        modelAndView.addObject("links", links);
        return modelAndView;
    }
    ...
```

The `getTeammate` method has the same `@Secured("ROLE_USER")` annotation as `getTeammates`, which indicates that you don't have to be an admin to look up a user. Toward the bottom of this method, we do look up the current user's list of roles via `SecurityContextHolder.getContext().getAuthentication().getAuthorities()`. With this list, we can use a Java 8 stream and a `anyMatch(p -> p.getAuthority().equals("ROLE_ADMIN"))` lambda expression to see whether the user has `ROLE_ADMIN`. If so, add the link to `editTeammate`.

> It's possible to replace `SecurityContextHolder.getContext().getAuthentication()` with something lighter. We can, instead, add `Authentication auth` as another argument to our Spring MVC method. Spring MVC will automatically supply this parameter, slimming down our code. The trade-off is that it will ripple through several of the other Spring MVC methods in our controller. Either option is fine. The choice for this book was governed by space limitations.

Regarding securing our whole application, we aren't quite done. So far, we have secured the backend. Our current templates will properly deny access if the user clicks on links they aren't authorized to use. However, a better user experience would be to remove links the user isn't authorized to use, making the frontend dynamically respond to the context of security.

To alter the HTML using security settings, add `thymeleaf-extras-springsecurity3` to `build.gradle` so that the `dependencies` section looks like this:

```
dependencies {
    compile("org.springframework.boot:spring-boot-starter-
    thymeleaf")
    compile("org.springframework.boot:spring-boot-starter-data-
    jpa")
    compile("org.springframework.boot:spring-boot-starter-
    security")
    compile("org.thymeleaf.extras:thymeleaf-extras-
    springsecurity3")
    compile("org.springframework.hateoas:spring-hateoas")
    compile("com.h2database:h2")
}
```

This Thymeleaf plugin adds extra security-based tags to Thymeleaf's dialect. It allows us to query various bits of a user's security context and customize the HTML, as we'll soon see.

With that extra library added, let's add a security headline at the top of every page. To do this, we first need to add another `<div>` fragment to `_links.html`:

```
<div th:fragment="security">

    <div>
        <span sec:authentication="name" /> has
        <span sec:authentication="authorities" />
        <form th:action="@{/logout}" method="post">
            <input type="submit" value="Sign Out"/>
        </form>
    </div>
    <hr />

</div>
```

Let's walk through this fragment and see what it's designed to do:

- Thymeleaf puts all security-based attributes inside the `sec` namespace. The `sec:authentication` attribute is a handle on the current user's authentication context. It's equivalent to the Java-based `auth` we just used.

- The `sec:authentication="name"` attribute retrieves the user's principal, which is commonly referred to as their username. In this example, the two defined users are `roy` and `phil`.

- The `sec:authentication="authorities"` attribute retrieves the user's list of authorities, that is, roles.

- We also have a tiny form with `th:action="@{/logout}"` and `method="post"` so that logouts are forced through CSRF handling. This prevents malicious users from logging out users.

- By wrapping both bits of security information inside `<span>` elements, we can turn this into a single line that is shown at the top.

With that in place, update `edit.html`, `teammate.html`, and `teammates.html` to pull in this new fragment, as shown in the following code:

```
<body>
    <div th:include="_links :: security" />
```

With these updates plugged in, let's run the app (`./gradlew bootRun`) and visit `http://localhost:8080/teammates`. From the get-go, we are logged in automatically with Spring Security's anonymous filter.

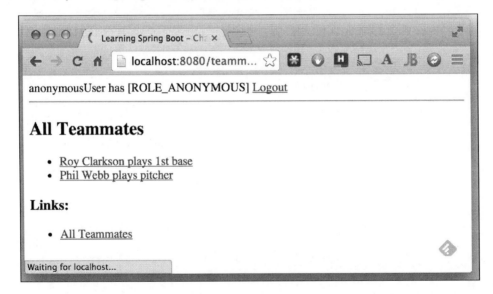

 You aren't really logged in. Instead, this is a placeholder for being unauthenticated . It's meant to avoid `NullPointerExceptions` for developers who don't supply the proper checks.

We can see the details about the anonymous user's credentials listed at the top. However, if we try to go any further, we will get redirected to Spring Security's built-in login form. Log in as `roy/clarkson`.

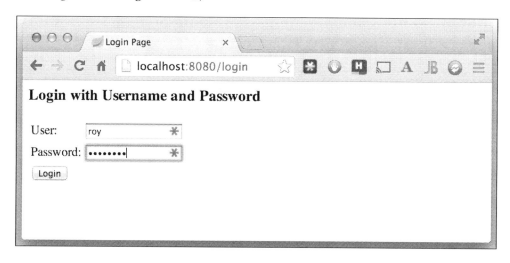

We can see Roy's username and roles as well as the logout link in the following output:

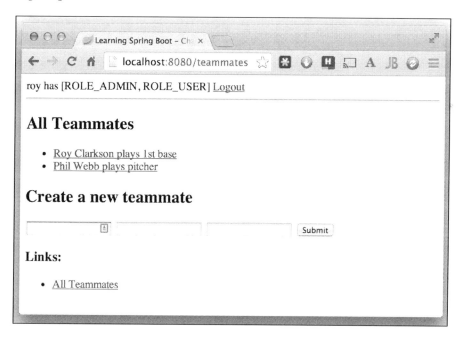

If we log out and then log back in as `phil`/`webb`, we see something different.

We can see that the new teammate form is gone. If we click on **Phil Webb** to look at his details, we see the following output:

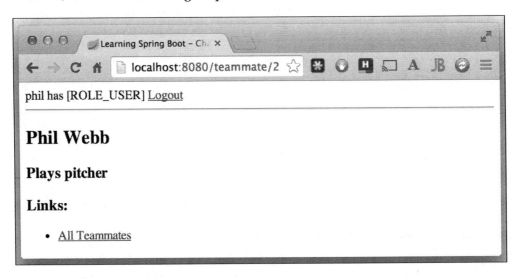

In this situation, the link to **Edit** is missing as well. The ultimate verification of security is if we attempt to access a page that we know exists but clearly isn't listed. Enter `http://localhost:8080/teammate/2/edit` in the browser's address bar, which is the path that is used to access the edit teammate page. You should see this:

Instead of seeing the edit page, we are redirected to an error page that displays **Access is denied**. A classic **403 Forbidden** page indicates that we are trying to reach something we aren't authorized for.

> The page shown is a fallback error page supplied by Spring Boot. To customize it, simply create `src/main/resources/templates/error.html` for Thymeleaf, or `error.ftl` for Freemarker, or create a custom controller that maps to `/error` and loads up a corresponding view.

We have just verified that Spring Security is applying both authentication and authorization to our application. This is a good place to also point out how Spring Security's default CSRF functionality is in full operation. If we look at the HTML source of `/teammates`, we can see this:

```
<form method="post" action="http://localhost:8080/teammates">
    <input type="text" id="firstName" name="firstName" value="" />
    <input type="text" id="lastName" name="lastName" value="" />
    <input type="text" id="position" name="position" value="" />
    <input type="submit" />
<input type="hidden" name="_csrf" value="f15f3bb5-ec87-447a-972a-
478ef36bd043" /></form>
```

The hidden _csrf value changes every session. The value supplied must match the value being held by the server for things to work. Obviously, this works here, because the form came from the server. If someone tried to hijack this form and reuse it, the server side will have rolled its CSRF value to a new one and will ultimately reject this false form.

> Remember, every form has this built in by default, which means login pages, teammate editing, and adding new teammates in our app has extra protection with no extra effort on our part.

Configuring user data to persist

So far, our configuration is quite extensive. We have created multiple accounts, with each user possessing different roles. However, this is an in-memory storage mechanism. To upgrade our app to support a complete production environment, we can borrow some of the concepts visited in *Chapter 4, Data Access with Spring Boot*. In that chapter we learned how to switch between an in-memory database and a persistent one using Spring Profiles. We'll do the same thing here and see what options Spring Security offers at the same time.

For starters, we need to add mysql-connector-java to build.gradle so that the dependencies section looks like the following code:

```
dependencies {
    compile("org.springframework.boot:spring-boot-starter-
    thymeleaf")
    compile("org.springframework.boot:spring-boot-starter-data-
    jpa")
    compile("org.springframework.boot:spring-boot-starter-
    security")
    compile("org.thymeleaf.extras:thymeleaf-extras-
    springsecurity3")
    compile("org.springframework.hateoas:spring-hateoas")
    compile("com.h2database:h2")
    compile("mysql:mysql-connector-java")
}
```

> Again, spring-boot-gradle-plugin will automatically supply the version number of this library, giving us one less thing to manage.

Now, let's assume the default profile, that is, no profile being specified, is our development environment. By default, if Spring Boot spots H2, HSQL, or Derby, it will automatically configure everything with a `create-drop` setting. This means that it will automatically create tables as required for our teammate data and drop them when the app shuts down.

In the previous section, we wrote `SecurityConfiguration.configureAuth()` to configure Spring Security's `AuthenticationManager` class with in-memory user accounts. As we are switching to profiles, let's rewrite that method as follows:

```
@Autowired
public void configureForDevelopment(AuthenticationManagerBuilder auth,
    Environment env) throws Exception {
    if (env.acceptsProfiles("!production")) {
        log.info("Setting up memory-based authentication for
        dev");
        auth.inMemoryAuthentication()
            .withUser("phil").password("webb").roles("USER").and()
            .withUser("roy").password("clarkson").roles("USER",
            "ADMIN");
    }
}
```

This has the same core functionality as before, except that a little bit extra functionality has been added. A Spring `Environment` object is autowired in addition to the original `AuthenticationManagerBuilder` class. This way, we can wrap the configuration with a profile check. The `env.acceptsProfiles("!production")` check ensures that we apply this in-memory user account setup only if we are not running the `production` profile.

We also need a configuration that supports the use of the `production` profile. So let's add this other method to `SecurityConfiguration`:

```
@Autowired
public void configureForProduction(AuthenticationManagerBuilder auth,
    DataSource dataSource, Environment env) throws Exception {
    if (env.acceptsProfiles("production")) {
        log.info("Setting up JDBC-based authentication for test
        database");
        auth.jdbcAuthentication().dataSource(dataSource);
    }
}
```

This method is autowired to receive both a `DataSource` object and an `Environment` object in addition to the `AuthenticationManagerBuilder` object. Let's break this down:

- It performs the same profile check, only this time it execute the configuration if we are running the `production` profile.

- To perform security checks against user data stored in a relational database, Spring Security uses JDBC, not Spring Data, to avoid adding extra dependencies. All it needs in order to find the appropriate user tables is `DataSource`.

 Let's stop for a second and clarify something. In the dev mode, we are using an H2 database, as found in the build file to store teammate data. We can configure Spring Security to use this database. We would simply have to plug in `auth.jdbcAuthentication().dataSource(dataSource).withDefaultSchema().withUser().password().roles().and()....` to `configureForDevelopment`. This setup would work identically to a functional perspective. However, I picked `inMemoryAuthentication()` to show the options that are available. When we switch to the `production` mode, there is no H2 database. Instead, we use MySQL to store everything, including teammate data and user data.

The rest of our `SecurityConfiguration` class is the same. This alone should demonstrate that the source of user data is independent of the security settings applied to the application.

You might be wondering why no user/password/role settings exist in `configureForProduction`. This is because we are using MySQL. Spring Security comes with a built-in `users.ddl` script that is used to configure some tables if you apply `.withDefaultSchema()` to `jdbcAuthentication()`. However, the dialect this script is written in doesn't work with MySQL. It's designed to support in-memory databases such as H2 and not persistent ones such as MySQL. As we are trying to preload data for a production setup, we can simply write our own SQL script to accommodate things.

We need to declare the tables in order to store users and authorities inside `src/main/resources/schema-mysql.sql`:

```
drop table if exists authorities;

drop table if exists users;
```

```
create table users (
  username varchar(50) not null primary key,
  password varchar(500) not null,
  enabled boolean not null);

create table authorities (
  username varchar(50) not null,
  authority varchar(50) not null,
  constraint fk_authorities_users foreign key(username)
  references users(username));

create unique index ix_auth_username on authorities
(username,authority);
```

Let's describe what's happening:

- Upon startup, the existing security-based tables are dropped if they exist.
- The `users` table contains `username`, `password`, and `enabled`.
- The `authorities` table contains a foreign key back to `users.username`. It also has an individual `authority` parameter, which is the same thing as a role.
- It also creates an index on `authorities`.

Again, I must stress that we are demonstrating the MySQL configuration but using this demo app to populate the content. In production, the user content would be managed by external means either through a controlled script or with a security ops user management tool that manages the user tables.

> This structure assumes the same as the defaults we have already seen in this chapter. But what if you need Spring Security to map onto a different, already existing schema? You can also configure custom SQL methods with `usersByUsernameQuery()`, `authoritiesByUsernameQuery()`, `groupAuthoritiesByUsername()`, and `rolePrefix()`. These extra configurations should support just about any setup. For more details, see `JdbcUserDetailsManagerConfigurer` (`http://docs.spring.io/spring-security/site/docs/current/apidocs/org/springframework/security/config/annotation/authentication/configurers/provisioning/JdbcUserDetailsManagerConfigurer.html`).

Next, we have to load some users and authorities. To do this, let's create `src/main/resources/data-mysql.sql` as shown:

```
insert into users
(username, password, enabled)
values
('roy', 'spring-android', true);

insert into users
(username, password, enabled)
values
('phil', 'spring-boot', true);

insert into authorities
(username, authority)
values
('roy', 'ROLE_USER');

insert into authorities
(username, authority)
values
('roy', 'ROLE_ADMIN');

insert into authorities
(username, authority)
values
('phil', 'ROLE_USER');
```

What can we see?

- We have the same two users: `roy` and `phil`. However, the passwords have been changed from the dev profile, so we can clearly see which set of users are active.
- The user `roy` has two authorities: ROLE_USER and ROLE_ADMIN.
- The user `phil` has one authority: ROLE_USER.

So, what does it take to load these two scripts? Again, *Chapter 4, Data Access with Spring Boot*, explains that Spring Boot will load `schema-${platform}.sql` and `data-${platform}.sql` files automatically using the Spring JDBC support. The only thing we need to do is declare the `${platform}` property and tie it to the `production` profile. To do this, we simply have to create `src/main/resources/application-production.properties` as follows:

```
spring.jpa.hibernate.ddl-auto=update

spring.datasource.platform=mysql
```

```
spring.datasource.url=jdbc:mysql://localhost/test
spring.datasource.username=your-username
spring.datasource.password=your-password
spring.datasource.driverClassName=com.mysql.jdbc.Driver
```

Spring Boot only loads this property file when `SPRING_PROFILES_ACTIVE=production` is defined. What all is there in this file? Take a look:

- First of all, we have it configured with the `update` mode, which means that it will create all the tables as required. This applies both to user tables and the `teammate` table.

- It also defines `platform` as `mysql`, which is the value required to load `schema-mysql.sql` and `data-mysql.sql`.

- Finally, it includes connection information in order to access our MySQL database.

 You must include the proper URL, username, and password information to connect to your own MySQL database.

A side effect of using a persistent database instead of H2 is that data, well, persists! If we kept running this app over and over to test out various features, our `DatabaseLoader` class will keep adding the same initial set of teammates repeatedly. If we make a slight alteration, as follows, this issue can be avoided:

```
@PostConstruct
private void initDatabase() {
    teammateRepository.deleteAll();

    Teammate roy = new Teammate("Roy", "Clarkson");
    roy.setPosition("1st base");
    teammateRepository.save(roy);

    Teammate phil = new Teammate("Phil", "Webb");
    phil.setPosition("pitcher");
    teammateRepository.save(phil);
}
```

The preceding file contains one extra line of code: `teammateRepository.deleteAll()`.

The `deleteAll` method is something that should probably never be used in real production code. However, when it comes to setting up a demonstration, it's great at cleaning out old data in order to prep for new data. In truth, the entire `DatabaseLoader` service should probably be wrapped with `@Profile("!production")` to avoid autoloading any data when this app is run in production. It has simply been left intact here to allow us to demonstrate MySQL support.

Configuring embedded Tomcat to use SSL

So far, we have built up an application with method-level security, alternate profiles of dev and production configuration, and wired up a MySQL server with Spring Security data loaded through Spring Boot scripts. The final touch to make our application secure from end to end would be to switch on SSL in the embedded Tomcat server.

Security is a multilevel process. Protecting assets with username / password / role controls is inadequate if anyone can snoop the network and steal credentials. Let's see how to prevent this.

The following class, `SecureTomcatConfiguration`, shows us how to create two Tomcat connectors. One is for unsecured HTTP on port 8080, and the other is for secured HTTPS on port 8443:

```
package learningspringboot;

import java.io.FileNotFoundException;

import org.apache.catalina.connector.Connector;
import org.apache.coyote.http11.Http11NioProtocol;
import org.springframework.boot.context.embedded.*;
import org.springframework.boot.context.embedded.tomcat.*;
import org.springframework.context.annotation.Bean;
import org.springframework.context.annotation.Configuration;
import org.springframework.util.ResourceUtils;
```

```
@Configuration
public class SecureTomcatConfiguration {

    @Bean
    public EmbeddedServletContainerFactory servletContainer()
            throws FileNotFoundException {
        TomcatEmbeddedServletContainerFactory f =
                new TomcatEmbeddedServletContainerFactory();
        f.addAdditionalTomcatConnectors(createSslConnector());
        return f;
    }

    private Connector createSslConnector() throws
    FileNotFoundException {
        Connector connector = new
        Connector(Http11NioProtocol.class.getName());
        Http11NioProtocol protocol =
                (Http11NioProtocol)connector.getProtocolHandler();
        connector.setPort(8443);
        connector.setSecure(true);
        connector.setScheme("https");
        protocol.setSSLEnabled(true);
        protocol.setKeyAlias("learningspringboot");
        protocol.setKeystorePass("password");
        protocol.setKeystoreFile(ResourceUtils
            .getFile("src/main/resources/tomcat.keystore")
            .getAbsolutePath());
        protocol.setSslProtocol("TLS");
        return connector;
    }

}
```

Let's break down this configuration:

- The new TomcatEmbeddedServletContainerFactory() expression creates
  the default Spring Boot embedded Tomcat container. This runs with the
  standard 8080 port and service unsecured content over HTTP.

- The addAdditionalTomcatConnectors(createSslConnector())
  expression adds another Tomcat connector. In this case, it delegates
  to a private method that is used to declare a secured one on port 8443
  over HTTPS.

The details of the secured connector are shown in the following table:

Method	Description
`setPort(8443)`	Sets the secured port to 8443
`setSecure(true)`	Secures the connection
`setScheme("https")`	Sets expected URI prefix to `"https"`
`setSSLEnabled(true)`	Turns on SSL for this connector
`setKeyAlias("learningspringboot")`	Specifies the key's username, used when looking in the keystore file
`setKeystorePass("password")`	Specifies the key's password inside the keystore file
`setKeystoreFile("src/main/resources/tomcat.keystore")`	Provides a path to the keystore file where the certificate that encrypts packets is to be found
`setSslProtocol("TLS")`	Use the industry standard TLS/SSL combination of security encryption to secure traffic

We're not done until we create a certificate that Tomcat can use to sign, authenticate, encrypt, and decrypt with. TLS/SSL is based on X.509 certificates, and this requires that we create a keystore file. Assuming that we have a shell open in the same folder as build.gradle, we can do this by typing the following:

```
$ keytool -genkey -alias learningspringboot -keyalg RSA -keystore src/
main/resources/tomcat.keystore
Enter keystore password: password
Re-enter new password: password
What is your first and last name?
  [Unknown]:  Learning Spring Boot
What is the name of your organizational unit?
  [Unknown]:  Packt
What is the name of your organization?
  [Unknown]:  Packt
What is the name of your City or Locality?
  [Unknown]:  IoT
What is the name of your State or Province?
  [Unknown]:  Earth
What is the two-letter country code for this unit?
  [Unknown]:  US
```

```
Is CN=Learning Spring Boot, OU=Packt, O=Packt, L=IoT, ST=Earth, C=US
correct?
  [no]:  yes


Enter key password for <learningspringboot>
    (RETURN if same as keystore password): <RETURN>
```

What is happening?

- `-genkey`: This asks keytool to create a new public/private key.

- `-alias learningspringboot`: This is our username and should line up with `setKeyAlias`. A keystore can have more than one alias, but we only need one in this situation.

- `-keyalg RSA`: This is the algorithm that is used to generate the public/private key.

- `-keystore ...`: This is the path to store our new key. We are embedding this keystore inside the application for use at runtime.

> keytool is a command-line tool provided by the JDK. It's available on any platform where you have installed Java for development purposes. keytool can also be used to import keys generated elsewhere. For example, it's possible to purchase a certified key from many ISP or DNS providers and import it into your application's keystore.

> Do not publish, release, or otherwise disclose this keystore to the public. It contains the private key used by our application. While the key is password-protected, a brute force attack can result in a complete breach of security. Do not use the key aliases and key passwords shown in this book. Use a strong, cryptographically secure password generator and don't forget to lock up these files against outside access. We are showing you the keystore pass inside the code, but as was shown throughout this book, you can inject it via `@Value()` annotations to keep it out of your source code.

We are almost done. The last step is to tune our security policy such that any and all requests to the site are redirected to a secure channel:

```
@Override
protected void configure(HttpSecurity http) throws Exception {
    http
```

```
            .authorizeRequests()
                .antMatchers(HttpMethod.GET, "/teammates").permitAll()
                .anyRequest().authenticated()
                .and()
            .requiresChannel()
                .anyRequest().requiresSecure()
                .and()
            .formLogin()
                .defaultSuccessUrl("/teammates")
                .and()
            .logout()
                .logoutSuccessUrl("/teammates");
    }
```

So, what's different? We added `requiresChannel().anyRequest().`
`requiresSecure()` to force any and all traffic to be redirected over a secure channel.

 By default, Spring Security redirects traffic from port 80 to port 443, and port 8080 to port 8443. For any other port configurations, you will have to add `portMapper().http(/unsecured port/).` `mapsTo(/secured port/)` into the chain of configuration shown.

With this all this in place, let's start things up and see what happens! Just type `./gradlew bootRun`. After the lengthy start up sequence, we should see something like this at the end:

```
2014-08-25 11:33:29.728 ... : Tomcat started on port(s): 8080/http 8443/
https
```

This indicates that the application is listening on both 8080 (unsecured HTTP) as well as 8443 (secured HTTPS).

 What about hosting my embedded Tomcat server behind a secured Apache web server with SSL termination? This is a popular configuration where the app itself doesn't need SSL, but the environment (PaaS or any other) does offer SSL. Spring Boot comes with built-in support for traditional HTTP headers **x-forwarded-for** and **x-forwarded-proto**. You simply have to add `server.tomcat.remote_ip_` `header=x-forwarded-for` and `server.tomcat.protocol_` `header=x-forwarded-proto` to `application.properties`. See `http://docs.spring.io/spring-boot/docs/1.1.6.RELEASE/` `reference/htmlsingle/#howto-enable-https` for more details.

Spring Security's default web-level protections

Remember how we earlier mentioned the extra security headers that Spring Security provides? Let's pause for a moment and check them out from the command line using `curl`:

```
$ curl -i localhost:8080/teammates
HTTP/1.1 302 Found
Server: Apache-Coyote/1.1
Location: https://localhost:8443/teammates
Content-Length: 0
Date: Wed, 27 Aug 2014 01:17:02 GMT
```

From this, we can see a 302 redirect to the secured SSL address, `https://localhost:8443/teammates`. Let's follow that and try again:

```
$ curl -i -k https://localhost:8443/teammates
HTTP/1.1 302 Found
Server: Apache-Coyote/1.1
X-Content-Type-Options: nosniff
X-XSS-Protection: 1; mode=block
Cache-Control: no-cache, no-store, max-age=0, must-revalidate
Pragma: no-cache
Expires: 0
Strict-Transport-Security: max-age=31536000 ; includeSubDomains
X-Frame-Options: DENY
Set-Cookie: JSESSIONID=2DF972B5847F02C6A90778FE12A8619D; Path=/; Secure; HttpOnly
Location: https://localhost:8443/login
Content-Length: 0
Date: Wed, 27 Aug 2014 01:17:43 GMT
```

This time, we added `-k` to avoid certificate verification, as it's self-signed. Several things are supplied by Spring Security by default, and they are shown as follows:

- `X-Content-Type-Options: nosniff`: This is a header that is used to tell the browser to avoid sniffing MIME types when none is provided. This prevents people from hiding malicious JavaScript inside seemingly harmless files such as a PostScript document.

- `X-XSS-Protection: 1; mode=block`: This signals the browser to block anything that appears to be a reflected XSS attack.

- `Cache-Control: no-cache…`, `Pragma: no-cache`, and `Expires: 0`: This instructs the browser to clear out and not cache secured content, preventing a follow-up user from accessing a previous user's secured content from the browser's cache.

- `Strict-Transport-Security`: This helps protect us from cases where people enter a website's URL but leave out `https`, opening the door to potential man-in-the-middle attacks. HSTS headers direct the browser to assume that after visiting a site's HTTPS URL, all future visits to this site will assume the same. It's important to remember that HSTS only works if the browser trusts the app's certificate. This means that self-signed certificates (like the one we set up) won't work.

- `X-Frame-Options: DENY`: This tells the browser to not allow our website to be hosted inside a frame. This mitigates the risk of clickjacking (`https://www.owasp.org/index.php/Clickjacking`) where a user might click on something that is not a secured asset.

Spring Security does a good job of providing support for highly adopted security standards.

Navigating our fully secured app

Let's see what happens if we enter the unsecured `http://localhost:8080/ teammates` address into the browser's navigation bar.

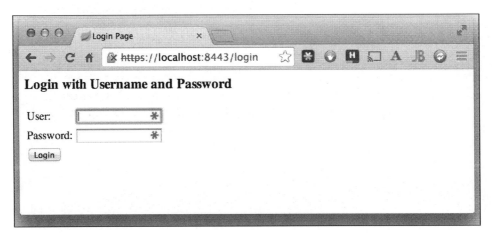

The application has automatically redirected us to `https://localhost:8443/teammates`. Let's proceed to log in as Roy.

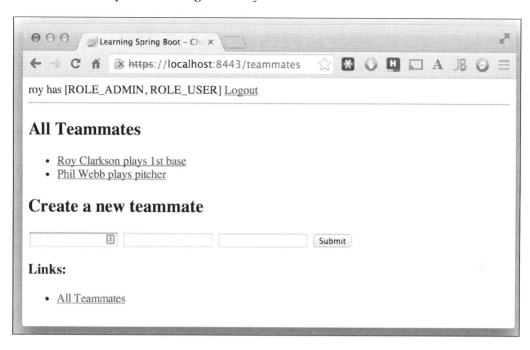

We can now see that the application itself is serving everything over SSL.

> We created a self-signed certificate. It is highly likely that you will see a warning page the first time you visit this site. You must pick either **Proceed Anyway** (or the equivalent for your browser) or run the site with a certificate purchased from a vendor instead.

With all of this, our application is now strongly secured using widely accepted, standardized security headers. We are running it in dev mode, but we can easily switch over to the `production` mode and expect the same results but with a different set of users.

Summary

In this chapter, we created a functional website in order to manage a team roster. Then we added Spring Security and configured a policy of form authentication, role authorization, and method-level security. We configured two different profiles, one for dev and one for production, so that we could work with two different sets of users. Finally, we figured out how to create our own certificate and configure an SSL-based embedded Tomcat servlet container. We tuned Spring Security to force all traffic to go over the secured connection.

This is just the beginning. We didn't have room to learn about Spring Boot's support for things such as AMQP, WebSocket, Spring Batch, AOP, Project Reactor, and more. Hopefully, I've whetted your appetite to go out and discover what else Spring Boot has to offer.

Index

C

Cache Control 201
clickjacking
  URL 226
Cloud Foundry
  deploying to 70-75
  URL 70
Command Line Interface (CLI) tool 8
ConnectionFactory instance 105
constructor injection 52
CORS
  reference link, for configuration 32
counters 35
CRaSII
  URL 32, 123
  reference link, for commands 38
  used, for detailed management 36, 37
CrudRepository interface
  count() method 139
  deleteAll() method 139
  delete(ID id) method 139
  delete(Iterable<? extends T> entities)
      method 139
  delete(T entity) method 139
  exists(ID id) method 139
  findAll() method 139
  findOne(ID id) method 139
  save(Iterable<S> entites) method 139
  save(S entity) method 139
CSRF (Cross-site Request Forgery) 200, 201
custom CRaSH commands
  creating 123-130
custom health check
  writing 103-106
customized app data
  adding, to /info 106-111
custom metrics
  creating, for tracking message
      traffic 112-114

D

dashboard command 37
data
  loading programmatically 146-152
  loading, SQL script used 142-146

DatabaseLoader class 186
default web-level protections 225
deleteAll method 220
dependencies
  h2 183
  spring-boot-starter-data-jpa 183
  spring-boot-starter-thymeleaf 183
  spring-hateoas 183
domain model
  defining 183-185

E

editTeammate method 191
embedded Tomcat
  configuring 220-223
empty project
  creating, with start.spring.io 40
entities
  defining 135-141

G

gauges 35
getTeammate method 191
getTeammates method 190
GitHub
  access token, creating 50-55
  issues, fetching 48-50
  URL 50
GPars
  about 79
  URL 79
gradle-git plugin
  URL 108
Gradle project
  URL 182
gradlew (gradle wrapper) 54
Groovy enVironment Manager (GVM)
  URL 14
Groovy Grape
  URL 10
Groovy's JsonSlurper
  reference link 34
Groovy's power assertions
  reference link 19
groovy-templates package 10
group ID 11

Thank you for buying
Learning Spring Boot

About Packt Publishing

Packt, pronounced 'packed', published its first book "*Mastering phpMyAdmin for Effective MySQL Management*" in April 2004 and subsequently continued to specialize in publishing highly focused books on specific technologies and solutions.

Our books and publications share the experiences of your fellow IT professionals in adapting and customizing today's systems, applications, and frameworks. Our solution based books give you the knowledge and power to customize the software and technologies you're using to get the job done. Packt books are more specific and less general than the IT books you have seen in the past. Our unique business model allows us to bring you more focused information, giving you more of what you need to know, and less of what you don't.

Packt is a modern, yet unique publishing company, which focuses on producing quality, cutting-edge books for communities of developers, administrators, and newbies alike. For more information, please visit our website: www.packtpub.com.

About Packt Open Source

In 2010, Packt launched two new brands, Packt Open Source and Packt Enterprise, in order to continue its focus on specialization. This book is part of the Packt Open Source brand, home to books published on software built around Open Source licenses, and offering information to anybody from advanced developers to budding web designers. The Open Source brand also runs Packt's Open Source Royalty Scheme, by which Packt gives a royalty to each Open Source project about whose software a book is sold.

Writing for Packt

We welcome all inquiries from people who are interested in authoring. Book proposals should be sent to author@packtpub.com. If your book idea is still at an early stage and you would like to discuss it first before writing a formal book proposal, contact us; one of our commissioning editors will get in touch with you.

We're not just looking for published authors; if you have strong technical skills but no writing experience, our experienced editors can help you develop a writing career, or simply get some additional reward for your expertise.

Spring MVC Beginner's Guide

ISBN: 978-1-78328-487-0   Paperback: 304 pages

Your ultimate guide to building a complete web application using all the capabilities of Spring MVC

1. Carefully crafted exercises, with detailed explanations for each step, to help you understand the concepts with ease.

2. You will gain a clear understanding of the end-to-end request/response life cycle, and each logical component's responsibility.

3. Packed with tips and tricks that will demonstrate the industry's best practices on developing a Spring-MVC-based application.

Spring Web Services 2 Cookbook

ISBN: 978-1-84951-582-5   Paperback: 322 pages

Over 60 recipes providing comprehensive coverage of practical real-life implementations of Spring-WS

1. Create contract-first Web Services.

2. Explore different frameworks of Object/XML mapping.

3. Secure Web Services by authentication, encryption/decryption, and digital signature.

Please check **www.PacktPub.com** for information on our titles

open source

community experience distilled

Spring Data

ISBN: 978-1-84951-904-5   Paperback: 160 pages

Implement JPA repositories with less code and harness the performance of Redis in your applications

1. Implement JPA repositories with lesser code.

2. Includes functional sample projects that demonstrate the described concepts in action and help you start experimenting right away.

3. Provides step-by-step instructions and a lot of code examples that are easy to follow and help you to get started from page one.

Spring Security 3.1

ISBN: 978-1-84951-826-0   Paperback: 456 pages

Secure your web applications from hackers with this step-by-step guide

1. Learn to leverage the power of Spring Security to keep intruders at bay through simple examples that illustrate real-world problems.

2. Each sample demonstrates key concepts allowing you to build your knowledge of the architecture in a practical and incremental way.

3. Filled with samples that clearly illustrate how to integrate with the technologies and frameworks of your choice.

Please check **www.PacktPub.com** for information on our titles

Made in the USA
Lexington, KY
13 January 2016